MW01114357

No More Assholes

Your 7 Step Guide to Saying Goodbye to Guys and Finding
the Real Man You're Looking For

Chantal Heide

Chantal Heide www.canadasdatingcoach.com

Ordering Information:
Quantity sales. Special discounts are available on quantity purchases by corporations, associations, and others. For details, contact the publisher at the address above.

Printed in Canada Chantal Heide.
No More Assholes – Your 7 Step Guide to Saying Goodbye to Guys and Finding the Real Man You're Looking For / Chantal Heide
p. cm.

ISBN 13 - 978-153299683
ISBN 10 - 153299681
1. Family and Relationships —Dating Fifth Edition

14 13 12 11 10 / 10 9 8 7 6 5 4 3 2 1

ii

Other books by Chantal Heide

For Dennis Heide, my 12 out of 12

Contents

Acknowledgements

For the past eight years I've known there was a book waiting inside of me, and I'm grateful to finally see it come to light.

I want to thank the Internet for its wealth of resources and easily found second-hand textbooks, allowing me to educate myself thoroughly on a budget.

My parents for their endless patience and acceptance.

Catherine Muss for editing furiously under the tight deadline I put us under.

My amazingly helpful beta readers who kept me on the right track.

My strong tribal women, without whom I wouldn't be the woman I am today and who taught me to Shhhhhh….just let it happen.

My beautiful step children for adding an element in my life that I would otherwise never be able to savour.

My fur babies for balancing my work with play, cuddles, and welcome distractions.

Derek Murphy for creating a brilliant book cover, and Sheri at IC Publishing for her patience and help.

And of course, my husband, for growing with me so I could learn what intimate love, support, friendship, and a functional relationship is all about.

No More Assholes

Foreword

"No more assholes!" These are the words that came out of my mouth, proclaimed in a moment of frustration at the cycle of unsatisfying relationships ending in tears and heartbreak. I was 28 and done with learning what love shouldn't be. I realized then I'd suffered enough lessons on what sort of guy to stop falling for and was ready for my next evolution: learning what it meant to be loved for who I am.

Looking back on everything I've learned, what I really meant was, no more guys. Guys who weren't ready, willing, or able to be devoted to me and my happiness, Guys who were more focused on instant gratification than building a life together. What I was finally ready for was a Man, someone kind, steady, stable, and able to be my rock while rocking my world.

No More Assholes is not just the result of 20 years spent passionately studying human behaviour. It's also written from my perspective of 12 years in the trenches, learning what not to do and an additional 15 learning how to have a functional relationship with someone who sincerely cares for me, is devoted to me, and loves me for me.

This book not only teaches you how to transform your dating outcome so you stop wasting time with Guys, it teaches you how to help Guys who sincerely love you grow into the Man you need - or walk away from those who don't care to.

It's time to understand that the path to real love lies right in the palm of your hand.

It takes strong Women to create a world filled with strong Men.
Let's do this, together.

If You Haven't Done This Already, Out With The Old

> Until you purge and mend your broken heart, love can't find its way inside you. We are born in love, but through a lifetime of curve balls we sometimes lose touch with that innate emotion within us. Heal yourself, and love will blossom once again.

I WAS BROKEN-HEARTED. Even though the last few years had left us battle scarred and weary from trying to work through our emotional baggage, I wasn't ready to throw in the towel. But there it was, an e-mail saying it was over. My heart sank, but I kept calm and dialed his number.

He picked up the phone. "Hey." "Are you sure?" I asked quietly. "Yes," he replied.

"That's too bad."

It was all I had left to say. I had fought for us for so many years, and I was tired of being the glue that held our relationship together. He'd been distant for so long, but now he was voicing certainty he didn't want to be with me, and I needed to let him go. Wasn't he the one who'd taught me the lesson, "I don't want to be with anyone who doesn't want to be with me?"

I felt resignation, overwhelmed by the empty feeling there was nothing left for us. What option did I have? I was fatigued, spent of all my energy.

Or so I thought.

After a week, unable to shake the sense that his fate was still interlaced with mine I picked up my laptop and googled how to win him back. There was a connection beyond anything I'd ever experienced, and I feared losing all the little ways he complemented me. For the first time I'd found someone who could handle the amount of affection I needed to share. Could anyone ever kiss me as well, or be as perfect a fit when we spooned? The feeling I had when we held each other was out of this world, his energy seeming to vibrate pure love despite his distance, his anger, and his frustrations. Had I truly found a unicorn, or could there be another man out there who could be even better than this one?

I realized it was a chance I had to take. I had no choice but to stop mooning over someone who wouldn't commit to my happiness. To stop thinking all that was missing from my life were the increasingly rare good moments we had shared. To remember what didn't work, what made me unhappy, what felt disrespectful, and what I never, ever, wanted to have to deal with again. I had to learn how to start getting mad so that I could stop feeling sad.

Intuitively feeling this was the right direction for me, I started implementing steps to get myself out of this misery. Each time my head started spinning I put a leash on my poodle Maggie and walked to air out my mind and get my psyche moving forward. I started re-directing my thoughts from poor me, poor us, to *what the fuck*? I developed a new mantra: a strong and resolute *Fuck You!* which helped turn my emotional tides every time I found myself missing him and wanting to call.

All this began to strengthen me, creating a resolve that I would never put myself in a similar position with another man again. No longer would I be in a relationship where important events were swept under the rug. No longer would I accept coming in at fourth place on his list of priorities. No longer would I be with someone who told me my feelings didn't matter. No longer would I be with a man who placed all blame on me without taking an ounce of responsibility for his role in our fights.

I was done. Brush my hands together and walk away. Done.

I purged my house of everything that was us. All the little notes, photos, and workbooks from our couples therapy were packed up and left for him outside my front door. I deleted the pictures of us from Facebook, and as I purged every corner of my home of his presence I felt my soul start to soar and sing with the joy of starting over. I was open and ready for a new adventure, and as the new me began anticipating the next phase, I started to feel happy again. A weight was coming off, bit by bit.

I realize now what I was cleaning out was my willingness to accept a future where I was unhappy. I was sending a clear signal to the Universe what I did and didn't want, and it responded accordingly. In the end I got the man I was looking for, the one who loved and married me, and made all my dreams come true. By clearing my physical and emotional house I made space for true love to come in and set up headquarters. In essence, I finally took control of my destiny and said *yes* to happiness.

CHAPTER 1

Purge Your Last Relationship FIRST

IN ORDER TO FULLY COMMIT TO MOVING FORWARD you have to emotionally leave behind what doesn't serve you. Loving someone who won't make the effort to work through issues isn't serving you. Wanting to be with someone who doesn't commit to being a part of your growth isn't serving you. Staying with someone who is abusive in any form definitely isn't serving you.

But now, right now, you need to make a decision to serve yourself. You need to resolve to let go of anything that makes you unhappy and choose to embrace a new you, one who fundamentally understands that love is a verb, found in actions rather than words. Realize that the first decision on the road to lasting love is committing to doing what serves your own emotional and mental happiness first, because ultimately no one can love you more than you love yourself.

So what does that mean?

It means caring enough about yourself to create boundaries, saying goodbye to guys who aren't willing to work on a relationship and opening yourself up to being with a man who'll love and cherish you. Since real men aren't attracted to women who don't love themselves, it means making your own happiness a priority. And it means focusing on your peace of mind first and viewing a relationship as the icing on your cake, seeking a partner who views you as valuable a prize he worked hard to obtain.

Know that the Universe works in amazing ways; always bringing you what you're ready for. If your heart is still attached to the last guy you broke up with, the Universe knows you're not ready for something better. Even if it did bring you what you need, you'll reject that gift because you'll be blind to it. You need to see the bigger picture and realize that when you're prepared for more it's out there, waiting for you. But nobody can see the door leading into a perfect garden if they're standing a foot away from the wall; step back far enough to see the doorway to happiness and love and walk through.

But first, how do you walk away from your past and clear your emotional space for something better? Here are 5 steps that will get you on the right track.

Step 1 – Get Out, and Get It Out

Step out into Mother Nature, and take a deep breath. There's so much more waiting for you out in this world, but you won't see it until you get outside and beyond the spinning thoughts in your head. Part of you may want to just curl up and mourn the sweet moments you shared and the life you'd imagined together, but you need to do the opposite right now. Open your senses and go experience the beauty in nature. Find it in the rough bark of a tree, in the wind whispering through leaves, in the birdsong all around you, in the sweet smell of gardens, in the cute dogs and friendly people you'll encounter on walks. Mother Nature contains some serious healing properties for your soul; tap into her!

The University of Kyoto published a study in 2007 (1) detailing how time spent in forests reduced feelings of hostility and depression, while significantly increasing feelings of liveliness. Even hospitals are creating gardens in response to a study published by Roger Ulrich in 1984 (2) suggesting that patients healed faster just by looking at nature through their windows. So be proactive in your emotional healing by getting out and taking advantage of your local parks and trails. Don't build walls of sorrow around your heart that a good man won't be able to penetrate.

Make sure you go see your friends, or make new ones; get out, be social, and start a new social habit, avoiding activities that keep you sitting home alone. We're social creatures by nature, and given that our penal system puts people in solitary confinement for committing the worst crimes or misbehaving in jail, doesn't it make sense to do the opposite for yourself? Don't make this time feel punitive; turn this into your moment to heal, right now. You've suffered enough. Surround yourself with people who care for you, who make you laugh, who excite your mind. Changing what's happening in your life helps change what's happening inside your head.

Cry. Cry, cry, cry. Cry every time you feel like it, and cry as hard as you want. Let it bend you in two, take you to the ground, and curl you up in a fetal position; let those tears come because they function as your emotional detox. Every tear you cry is a little drop of letting go of the guilt, the anger, the sadness, and the shame you accumulated during your last relationship and maybe from some of your previous ones too. Purge yourself emotionally, and don't stop until it's over. It may take a week, it may take a year, but don't suppress your tears, and don't beat yourself up for crying. Let it out. If you keep all your sorrow bottled in, there won't be any room left for love and happiness.

Your body and soul knows what you need to do, so open up and allow your feelings to flow. Every time you suppress your feelings you leave a little something to come fetch you later, something to bubble up and say, "Look at me, I'm still here." Don't. I remember at one point thinking, *I didn't cry today,* like it was a novelty. That's okay. It's okay to feel so low that every day has its moment where your emotions take you all the way down, as long as you really allow them to come out of your body and use measures to lift your spirits back up after. Eventually, there won't be any of those sad feelings left to purge, and the space that's left will fill with the love and good feelings you're working hard to create. Make that space for those amazing new feelings by letting go of the old ones.

Step 2 – Get Mad (Forgive the strong language, it's necessary for this step)

This is how I tell people to do this step; *Learn the art of Fuck you!* Those powerful words fuelled my growth from the meek girl who would accept sub-par behaviour to a woman who knew what was right (and wrong) for her. You already know there's no statement more powerful than *Fuck you!* for communicating what you won't stand for. Now, own your power and use these two words to stand up for what you know you deserve.

You want to override my feelings and act like they don't matter compared to yours?

Fuck you!

You want to be unfair with me?

Fuck you!

What frustrated you in your past relationships? Dig deep and come up with everything you never want to face again. Write each one down and be clear about what your future will no longer hold. If you miss his company, remember how he kept you in the dark about important matters. If you miss how he touched you, remember every time he felt miles away while sitting right beside you. If you miss the things he did for you, remember every time you asked for something and got shot down or every time you were even afraid to ask.

This is what gives you strength, and the more you stand your ground and use *Fuck you!* to avoid going backwards and ending up in the same drama you were dealing with before, the better it can help root you into your own personal power.

Every time he comes around and wants to talk you into getting back into the same relationship with him, *Fuck you!* helps you feel stronger and dig your roots deeper. And do you know what happens to the tree with roots that are firm and woven deep into Mother Earth? She becomes so strong that the scariest storm won't knock her over. She becomes so powerful that nothing fazes her anymore, and after every downpour she feeds off the rainwater and grows taller, more beautiful, and more capable.

When my ex-boyfriend came calling back, I took the *Fuck you!* I'd developed on my walks with Maggie and put it on the table.

You want to tell me how I'm wrong for feeling how I did?

"Fuck you!"

You want me to come back and be with you when nothing has changed?

"Fuck you!"

You have every finger pointed at me and none at yourself for the years of fights we had?

"Fuck you!"

Not only *Fuck you!* but leave me alone because I'd decided to move forward instead of swimming in the same muck filled water that had become our relationship. I was done being stagnant, trying to put the same ratty old bandage on the same gaping wound, and I was ready for a revolution, both within myself and in the direction my next relationship would take. I had learned a valuable lesson about what made me unhappy, and I would take this education and graduate to something better. No if's, and's, or but's. *Fuck You!*

The beauty of anger is the resolve it gives you to grow into a new person. When you create enough inner heat to fire yourself up and propel yourself forward, it's like a steam engine locomotive plowing down the track. Powerful, full of life and fire, your anger will give you the strength to find a new destination, leaving behind the old place full of hurt and frustration, and driving you towards the love you're seeking.

Step 3 – Purge Him Out of Your Life

It's not just emotional space you need to make; the physical space he holds in your life has a huge impact on your day-to-day thoughts. You need to get rid of those visual reminders that trigger unhappy memories. It's time to clear your personal space of him so you have plenty of space for the new you. Otherwise, you're just spinning in the same place, coming across reminders and dealing with interruptions to your growth when you get yanked backwards.

Get the pictures out of the frames, off the walls, and deleted on social media. Keep one in a shoe box because one day you'll be able to look back and say, "Yeah, I used to be there." But stash the box far away in the crawl space or the back of a closet shelf. The only time you need to think about the past is when you want to reflect on the lessons it taught you about how to better live your life.

His toothbrush, spare socks, and other whatnots can be boxed up and given back or thrown out. Same with those notes and cards and gifts he gave you that are nothing more than reminders of what was. More expensive items can be boxed and put away until their emotional attachment has faded, at which point you can use them for the items they are rather than the mementos they represented. If you bought furniture together and it's making you sad every time you look at it, replace it.

Clean up your house and clear it of his presence, and feel the process of consciously taking control of your life taking place. Be aware of each step you take and make it a victory, one more *out with the old, in with the new* mantra singing in your head. Play some kickass girl-power music, and dance and sing along with all your heart. Feel empowered as you do this, because you're taking back your life, your space, and your emotions. Own this moment!

Embrace growth. It hurts, but don't growing pains always hurt? Pain is okay; make friends with it because when done right pain is an indication of how far you're willing to go to become a better you. It's like working out to become stronger and fitter; you're literally tearing the muscle fibre, and it's the healing process that leaves you feeling sore as your body creates more muscle to fill the spaces you tore apart. Just remember, when you've healed you come back stronger and able to lift heavier loads, and true love requires a lot of strength.

Be willing to invest the work into becoming your next evolution, and remind yourself of the caterpillar who sheds its skin before creating the chrysalis from which it emerges as a beautiful butterfly. Make your home the sanctuary within which you transform yourself. Remind yourself that one day you'll share this space with the love of your life, and in order for him to feel fully welcomed the past needs to be cleared out. Prepare yourself today for what you want tomorrow: a home filled with loving memories, created with a man who adores and cherishes you.

Step 4 - Be a Yes Woman

If you're going through a tough breakup I understand if part of you wants to stay safely nestled in your home, but don't. When a friend asks you to go for coffee, say yes. Your workplace has a function? Say yes. When you get that housewarming invite on Facebook, say yes. You might end up saying yes to more invitations than you attend, but at least you're getting into the habit of saying yes to life. In time you'll be back on track and happily going out into the world, enjoying everything it offers.

But also, say yes to yourself. Be indulgent. What do you want to do? You've stepped out of a relationship where you were fracturing your desires, dividing them into categories: me, him, us. Now make it all about you. Take that class you've been dreaming of but didn't sign up for because it didn't involve him. Call up the friends you sidelined while you focused on your relationship. Make time for meditation, yoga, walks, making new friends, trying new things. It's time to learn what loving yourself is all about.

Make your satisfaction, your happiness, your life your number one priority. Now is the time to start this habit because the better you care for yourself, the better you can care for someone else when you fall in love again. The man you're looking for is seeking a whole woman, one who knows how to balance her needs with whatever else the world demands of her. Practice today what you'll be offering tomorrow, and when you meet him there'll be nothing intimidating for him to fix, only an abundance of qualities he can freely love.

Step 5 – Be Clear Going Forward

Every relationship is a learning experience, so learn from this one before seeking your next. If you don't, then it truly was time wasted. Think about what you loved, but also think about what you now know is a deal breaker, and plant the seed of *never again* in your brain. Life is as much about learning from mistakes so you can avoid repeating them as it is about learning what gives you pleasure so you can continue pursuing happiness. Learn, and become stronger and more certain of what you want from life and love. This clarity will help the Universe send you the right man next time because it responds to the signal from your heart. Choose the right frequency, and you'll see the perfect partner come your way.

When my ex broke up with me I took the time to really think about what I wanted, deep in my heart. When we started dating I was coming out of my first marriage and initially didn't think I wanted to get married all over again. "I just want symbolism. If we wear rings and call each other husband and wife, that'll be enough for me. I don't want to have another wedding," I told him, but over the years I found myself teary eyed and yearning each time I saw a romantic proposal on TV. Now that we weren't together anymore and I could re-write the rules, I realized I wanted to get married again.

I also became crystal clear on what level of communication I wanted, and I made a firm decision about what role I'd settle for in my next relationship. *I'll never be with a man who treats another woman better than me,* I vowed, experience having taught me how hard it was to come after a baby-mama. I needed to be honest with myself about my feelings and my own limitations.

Don't be afraid to raise your standards and create new rules. Fear is the most expensive emotion you can have, because it will cost you in the long run. Being afraid of losing somebody who's wrong for you will cost you time. It will cost you your self-esteem, because you'll diminish yourself in an attempt to accept a low standard. It'll cost you money, because you'll bend over backwards to appease him. It might even cost you your friends and family, because you'll want to surround yourself with people that make him happy. Don't be afraid of fear, be afraid of how fear can keep you from what you really want in a relationship.

When I didn't chase after him, my ex came back, offering the symbolism I'd wanted. But I'd grown, and now I wanted more in my next relationship. More communication, more commitment, and more devotion. I stood my ground, not because I was being stubborn, but because I had changed. I wasn't the same person anymore, and I was moving forward and looking for a relationship that matched my new emotional growth.

It could have gone one of two ways. He could have stayed the same person he was and found someone who would fit him again, or he could change too, and grow into the man I was now looking for. Either way, I would have been fine because I was committed to myself first, and a relationship second, and I was now looking to be with a man who would fit my newfound lifestyle and beliefs.

STEP 1

Grounding

Although Grounding is the last step I learned when it came to creating the perfect relationship, this step is by far the most important one. Like attracts like; if you're anxious and seeking a partner, you'll find an anxious man. If you're confident in yourself and happy, you'll find a confident, happy man. Ground yourself, and nothing short of magic happens in your existing and future relationships

CHAPTER 2

Open Mind, Open Heart, Open for Business

MY QUEST FOR GROUNDING opened my mind to a lot of wisdom and insight and yes, sometimes a little divine intervention. The most enlightening event I experienced took place around 20 years ago. It not only influenced my belief that self-discovery and self-confidence are game changers in life, but most importantly it showed me we can also connect with each other on a level runs deeper than our five senses.

It happened over a weekend at an intimate spiritual retreat nestled by the Richelieu River near Montreal. There, we surrendered our watches and committed to living entirely in the moment. We rose with the morning sunshine, went to bed long after sunset, and in between we learned to create a sanctuary deep inside our minds.

On our last night we found ourselves joined by past attendees, volunteers eager to share the magic they'd already discovered. I found myself paired with a former student who sat across from me, a small piece of paper in hand. On it, hidden from my eyes, was information about someone   I'd never met but who would play a part in opening my mind to my innate personal power. My stomach tingled with nervous excitement.

"Whenever you're ready" my partner said softly. I sat back in my chair, put my hands on my legs with my palms turned to the ceiling, and closed my eyes. Unguided for the first time, I began my descent into the sacred space in my mind, using the steps we'd learned over the past few days. In my mind's eye I made my way through a glowing rainbow, surrounding myself with each brilliant colour. Rays of red, orange, yellow, green, blue, indigo and violet ultimately transported me to a lush forest path. I walked forward and, arriving at a tiny house I had built, stood on the threshold and bathed myself in the brilliant white light radiating from above the wooded door. With my spirit now cleansed of any residual negativity, I turned the handle and walked into my spiritual home.

Inside I had created a cozy room with no discernible corners. To the left, gleaming bottles filled with rainbow colours lined the wall. They represented my medicine cabinet, each colour healing what I might need at any given time. Green infused me with unconditional love. Red was my source of confidence and security. Yellow filled me with self-worth and trust in myself. Orange, to inspire passion and creativity. Blue gave me the courage to communicate my creative expressions and personal truths while Indigo helped develop my insights. And finally, violet, to connect my spirit to what I call God or the Universe.

Before me rose a stage, and in front of that a homey white couch where I had watched my life's story unfold without judgement. I turned to the right and walked to an elevator with gleaming silver doors designed to bring in the essence of anyone I invited inside my house for the purpose of healing and communication.

Pausing in front of them, I took a moment to settle deeper into a meditative state and make sure I was open to whatever happened next.

"I'm ready," I said aloud. My partner read from the card, "His name is Michael Belyea. He is 31 and lives in Sutton."

Michael from Sutton, come in please, I said inside my mind. *I'm here, waiting to meet you.*

The elevator doors slid open and I watched as a man stepped out, a subtle glow emanating from his body. I moved forward and shook his hand, my physical hand moving up and down in the air while my spiritual hand shook his. "Hello," I said to him.

My task was to tell my partner what sickness this stranger had by touching his energy. Starting at his head, I raised my hands, again both in this world and in my mind, and held them an inch from his body. I felt his warm energy push against my palms while they patted the air in front of me, and I slowly traced the outline of his body. But as I passed over his left leg my hands suddenly slapped together, as though encountering a vacuum. Wham! I frowned in confusion.

"I don't know," I told my partner. "Try again," he said gently.

Once again I put my hands up, and as I touched Michael's energy I sensed the pressure return on my palms, though in the physical world all I seemed to do was pat the air in front of me. I got to his legs, and I reached his left shin. Wham!

"He's missing the bone below his left knee," I said out loud. It sounded weird, even to me, but it was the message my brain relayed.

"Are you sure?" my partner asked. "Yes," I said.

"Look." I opened my eyes, and the card turned around: 'Michael Belyea from Sutton, 31-years-old, left leg amputated below the knee.' My jaw dropped, and looking around the room I witnessed the same expressions of awe as the people with whom I'd shared this transformative weekend stared with wonder at the cards their partners held. Each card contained a different person with a different malady, and each of us had realized our own heightened abilities. At 24 I was the youngest person there, but age didn't matter. Life experience didn't matter. We stood as equals in that moment, each of us on a quest to awaken our spirits. We had all successfully grounded our own energies into something extraordinary.

I want to assure you that even though this was a personal experience, each and every one of us can achieve a deep connection between ourselves and another human being. The only question is, are you willing? Will you take down the barriers that keep you from creating a connection so strong that nothing, not even your physical bodies, can keep you apart? You can, but only if you step onto the path that will ultimately get you there.

CHAPTER 3

Eliminate Unnecessary Noise

YOU might be tempted to gloss over this section, but don't. Grounding is the first step to achieving the relationship you want because it helps you lay the proper foundation: a peaceful, loving, compassionate state of mind and an inner sense of happiness.

Way too often women (and men) look to relationships to give them the fulfillment they're seeking. But here's the thing. To get what you really want, you need to have a sense of that fulfillment first. I'm going to say this over and over, like attracts like, and you need to be what you're looking for to finally get what you desire. It's not hard, but it does require your commitment to focus inward and discover yourself on a deeper level.

When I coach women through these seven steps what I witness first is a transformation in their lives, an alignment of their ducks. Whatever is keeping them from feeling happy and settled, whether it's past trauma or their current career path, amazing things start to happen in those areas of their lives. Opportunities come forth in the form of better job offers or promotions, and nagging voices of self-doubt fade into the background, but it takes dedication. If you skip this step, you're skipping developing the most important traits needed to accomplish a great relationship. Grounding doesn't just help you through what's blocking you from being happy, satisfied, and empowered. It helps you effectively navigate relationships by reducing your willingness to fight and increasing your capacity to exhibit empathy and understanding, traits the man you're looking for will be grateful you exhibit. This is prep work, just like when you're cooking a fabulous meal; you need to spend time tending to the fine details before you can enjoy the outcome.

Take this section seriously and watch as everything falls into place.

Life is filled with static, mental noise pollution that's constantly bombarding us. It's in the conditioning we grew up in, which spins our perceptions about ourselves and the world we live in. It's delivered in the hurt we feel when sideswiped by someone else's baggage, a slap in the face echoing through generations of abuse and spewing outwards, trying to convince us we're not worthy of real love. It prowls through the messages that infiltrate our psyches from television, movies, billboards, and magazines, telling us we'll be good enough when we look and act the way they say we should. All of it is static, and its droning hum needs to be drowned out so we can connect to who we are fundamentally: beings built to experience the power of love.

And love doesn't reside in the noise, it's found in the quiet of our own hearts.

As babies we all laugh even if we've never seen or heard laughter, proving every one of us is born with joy already programmed into our DNA. Which begs the question: What other unseen traits do we possess? What if we were born with an inner compass, one that would always lead us to life's most rewarding challenges and greatest sources of love? I believe that if we quiet the static in our minds, we can begin to follow our own inner voice and guidance system towards our greatest fulfillment.

Your life is a projection of what you feel you deserve and can be nothing more, and experience has taught me that what we allow in our minds impacts what happens in our lives. I see negative people who find a problem for every solution living unhappy lives, and positive people who turn to self-improvement living rich and rewarding lives. When I reflect on the number of wealthy people entering rehab because a part of them can't imagine they deserve the good fortune they're experiencing, I realize it doesn't matter what you have; what matters is how you feel about what you deserve.

When you embrace the sense you deserve more, that you're worthy of what you want and are grateful for every little bit you get, you end up receiving more. By not subscribing to the belief that *I'll be happy when*, you create an opening for happiness inside your heart today. When you acknowledge each win, no matter how small, you actively train yourself to increase your ability to accept more goodness in your life, becoming part of the like attracts like law of attraction.

Think about Christopher Columbus. He set out to discover the world, not to *maybe* or *hopefully* discover something someone else hadn't. He was clear on his goal and confident in his ability to find the Far East. When you

cultivate mental clarity within the space you occupy, stretching your own power of creativity to create something beyond what you are experiencing right now, like Chris did, you set out on a path towards discovering something far better than what you're experiencing today.

Because you see, Dorothy, maybe just like that ability to laugh you were born with, you've been wearing those ruby red shoes for love all along. You've always had the ability to tap into your innermost desires and respond to them, so let me teach you how to click your heels and discover how amazing the space inside your head is. By being clear on who you truly are, you can imagine an achievable goal on where you're going to go from here.

First, let's talk about your capabilities. To define is divine, and the word capability means:

"Having power and ability; efficient; competent" (Thanks, Dictionary.com)

So what are we human beings actually capable of? We're capable of using our imagination to see something that isn't in front of us, like picturing ourselves lying on a sandy beach or imagining whether a dress will fit before trying it on. We're capable of forethought, the ability to see a future outcome, a great asset when deciding to not drink a bottle of wine and binge watch Netflix till 3 AM the night before a big meeting. It's by the grace of these qualities we find ourselves enjoying lush parks, towering skyscrapers, cell phones, and even parents. Because someone imagined a future different from the moment they lived in, something else was created, or something already created was improved upon. We all have these capabilities, and our power is   only

as strong as our desire to exercise them in a way that will improve our lives.

The key to unlocking your capabilities lies in learning to quiet the static interfering with them. If you're imagining the worst possible outcome, then worry is interfering with your ability to imagine a better life. If you let your brain run on its own train of thoughts with no input from you about what you'd really like to focus on, then you're essentially letting the monkeys run the zoo. And I can't find anyone who ever thought that was a good idea.

CHAPTER 4

Don't Let the Monkeys Run the Zoo

WHAT IF YOU LET your brain just do its own thing?

Physically, researchers have found that not focusing on creating your own brain ultimately means a less developed hippocampus, the region of your brain responsible for learning, memory, compassion, introspection, and self-awareness, and a more developed amygdala, the part of your brain that controls your fight or flight reactions and stress hormones.

When you let the monkeys run the zoo your mental focus tends to center on negativity instead of what can make your existence more harmonious. This is a natural and evolutionary aspect of our thinking patterns, since retaining negative outcomes has higher survival value than dwelling on the positives. But in today's world our needs are different, and we can free up more brain power and exercise greater control over how we function and hence better adapt to our current reality. We can turn that negative tendency around and become more desire/solution oriented instead of spinning in survival mode.

In 2011 Harvard published a study called *Eight Weeks To a Better Brain* (1). Researchers studied participants' brain scans before and after 8 weeks of meditating an average of 27 minutes a day. The end results showed an actual change in the physical makeup of the brain, notably a gain in grey- matter density in the hippocampus and a shrunken amygdala. In addition to that, the participants noted an increased sense of inner peace and a reduction of anxiety.

Having a larger amygdala worked great for us humans several thousand years ago when we were dodging saber-tooth tigers, flesh-eating kangaroos, and invading tribes. We needed a highly developed fight-or-flight response so we could be quick in our reactions and avoid becoming dinner. And while our amygdala is maybe smaller now, today's commonly reported high-stress levels tell me it's still bigger than necessary. It seems we still have brains geared for a jungle where we were more often the prey than the predator, yet we're now living much safer suburban lives. It makes little sense, and our brains are struggling to deal with our factual reality. Simply put, shrinking the amygdala helps us reduce our stress levels and allows us to better deal with everyday life.

And what happens when we increase grey-matter in our hippocampus? An increase in memory and a heightened ability to process our world, along with deeper insights and a greater capacity for compassion. Necessary qualities for creating the loving and functional relationships we want.

Since it's scientifically proven you hold the power to physically change your brain to better adapt to life, why wouldn't you want to? Developing a stronger hippocampus to help you juggle multitasking would certainly be helpful, right?

And if shrinking your amygdala helps you connect to a deeper sense of peace, wouldn't you want to sit down today and start meditating?

I remember when I first read about the Harvard study I felt I'd been delivered a gift from above. I was two weeks into starting my business; paper littered my home from the mad outpouring of ideas gushing out of me, and a million questions were lining up to be answered. I was overwhelmed by the process of breaking down large ideas into smaller details, and I was hitting my maximum stress load. When I discovered an article detailing the outcome of their study I immediately knew I'd found the answer. I thought to myself, *I definitely could use more brain matter* And here's what happened: As I meditated every day the ideas sorted themselves out, and solutions cut through problems like a hot knife through butter. I no longer felt overwhelmed with the amount of planning needed for the tasks each idea gave birth to, and not only did everything feel easier, but I became more cheerful and relaxed. I was even smiling at strangers more.

Those days where one thing after another went wrong began to feel more interesting than stressful, and I kept having moments where I'd realize how calm I felt despite delayed appointments and cars refusing to start when I was running late.

And then, something else happened. My relationship got better. My desire to fight basically left me as my fight-or-flight response drastically shrank. I even led the way to a more functional relationship with my hubby, showing him what leaving the past behind truly meant. I was living in the moment and focused on nothing but creating peace and love.

Think about what this would mean for your next relationship. What if all you experienced every day was kindness, love, and understanding? It's possible. I've experienced it, and I've helped it happen time and again. We are predictable when you play with our common elements, and with a little time and effort you'll achieve the same amazing results as those who have walked this path before you.

CHAPTER 5

Hey Baby, What's Your Frequency?

WE ARE ALL FREQUENCY, and like radio waves our vibes are constantly transmitting back and forth across space and infecting one another.

Think about how you feel when listening to music. Who hasn't felt happy and uplifted, or sometimes tearful when listening to certain songs on the radio? Is it the music, or the frequency of the tone that makes you emotional? While music seems to help people delve into their feelings, research has also shown the frequencies found in music have a measurable effect on everything, even plants. In 1973 Dorothy Retallack (2) wrote a book detailing her experiments at the Colorado Women's College, where she found that under varying musical conditions plants were behaving in clear ways, from thriving on Jazz to wilting under the sound of rock-and-roll. Even chickens get a kick out of the right frequency, producing bigger eggs on classical music, as discovered by Nova Scotia's youngest farmer, 15- year-old Thian Carman in 2014 (3). Thian experimented with music after learning dairy farmers played classical songs in the milking barns, believing it helped the cows relax and produce more milk.

Words have frequency too. One popular experiment was conducted by Dr. Masaru Emotos (4), who froze distilled water in different petri dishes and labelled each with its own written message. The dishes assigned words associated with positivity such as "I love you" and "I appreciate you" appeared to form intricate snowflake shapes when examined under a microscope, while those labelled "Hitler" and "I hate you" produced misshapen blobs.

You can choose whether you'll believe Dr. Emotos' research on words, but even if you don't it's hard to deny how they affect our own sense of inner peace. When was the last time you felt serene and loving while saying "I can't stand you!" You don't. But how do you feel when saying "You're wonderful" to someone, or hear those words directed towards you? Probably nice and warm and fuzzy. That's the power of frequency.

Now ask yourself, what words are you directing towards the woman in the mirror? Are you being loving with yourself, or critical? How you speak to yourself colours how you view the world, and how love is filtered into your consciousness. Begin by filling yourself with loving kindness, and you'll notice not only how much love is directed your way, but you'll increase the amount of love you attract. Now that's a cycle I can really get into.

CHAPTER 6

Using Frequency

IF FREQUENCY EFFECTS your overall wellbeing, how can you use it to help yourself day to day? The answer is found in what you say and what you listen to.

Let's start with the easiest part: What you listen to. There's a trend that's survived through the ages called chanting; traditional healers and religious monks have long practiced the belief that the frequency of chants and mantras can be used to cure a wide variety of conditions, from arthritis and smallpox, to anxiety and depression. In 2001 David Aldridge published his book, *Case Study Designs In Music Therapy (5)*, discussing music's ability to alter our brain function. Many studies support the notion that specific sound frequencies help achieve a Theta state of brainwave activity, where your brain functions in a relaxed state of reduced consciousness known as deep meditation.

Personally, I don't like hearing negative words like cancer because the more we infiltrate our psyche with negativity the more we vibrate at that frequency, increasing our odds of embodying that particular tone. So I spend time each day filling my being with words like love, gratitude, and appreciation, really feeling them in the core of my being and allowing them to fill my body, visualizing that feeling spilling out of me and leaking into those around me. Maybe that's why my husband is so happy with me. It certainly can't be hurting.

Be conscious of the music and words that surround you. Do they make you feel uplifted or sad? Pay attention to your feelings when music is playing and if you need to, switch it up to induce a positive effect on your emotional state. If you have people in your life who are negative about themselves and everything around them, limit your exposure because their negative frequency can affect yours. Protect your energy; it's yours to control.

This brings me to the next part of maintaining an ideal frequency: what's said. I remember a valuable lesson I learned in my 20s when I lived in Montreal with my roommate Lynn. We shared a friend, Liza, who studied at McGill University. One day Lynn said, "I can't stand being around Liza; she's so negative! She's like an emotional vampire."

It was the first time I'd heard that term, and it opened my eyes to the effect our words have on how other people feel around us. I decided right then I would monitor what came out of my mouth because the last thing I wanted was to be another emotional vampire. I started pausing between what I thought and what I said, giving myself a moment to evaluate my words and ask whether they were positive or negative. If they were nothing but the venting of a negative sentiment, I tossed them before they left my lips. If they were positive, I gave them a pass.

Soon I was known for my positivity, and I enjoyed my new reputation as That Positive Girl. Not only did I feel more cheerful by refusing to give negativity a chance to thrive, but those around me felt uplifted by the positive vibes I created. My frequency was bouncing off them, changing theirs for the better, then bouncing back at me and making me feel great.

You can do this too. I know it takes practice, but trust me, every little bit counts. I'm not perfect and still don't catch myself every time, but you can make a significant impact on the amount of negativity you put out. Words, because their inherent sound carries frequency, have a lot of power, so choose them wisely and lovingly. Be strategic in your speech, and your frame of mind will follow suit.

Never reject yourself, no matter what you think. If you believe your hair looks crappy today, there's no need to dwell on it or try to convince everyone around you. The people who love you see you in a positive light already; don't dim their view by throwing a dark, wet blanket on their way of perceiving you. Let them love you and see you as beautiful and allow that love to shine deep inside of you. Negative words tend to build a barrier between you and love, and there are enough obstacles to overcome already. So next time you hear your brain telling you you're not pretty enough today, or you're not good or talented enough, shhhhhhh… Just let love happen.

CHAPTER 7
Awakening Your Heart Frequency

DID YOU KNOW your heart has a high frequency and is the part of you that's most awake and in tune with your surroundings? Numerous studies (6) have suggested that your heart even has a one to ten second pre-cognitive ability to predict the future and feed your brain information it needs to react to situations.

How did they figure this out?

Time and again researchers placed participants in front of monitors viewing images that were neutral or emotional while their physiological responses were observed. Lo-and- behold, even before the randomized images appeared the subjects' hearts would react, followed by the brain. Whoa.

Now, if emotional information can travel between the brain and the heart, why wouldn't it travel outward as well? Haven't you been around someone and thought, *Gee, what a stinking dark cloud coming off that person.* Or have you ever had someone come into a room and suck the happiness right out of it? How about the opposite? Do you know anyone who can brighten a room just by entering it? A friend who makes you happier by just being around? That's their heart energy.

And how would you like people to feel when you're around? Think about that. You can have any impact you want; it's simply a matter of deciding to develop your emotional energy through meditation and mind-changing words, laying the foundation for a more loving exchange between you and everyone around you.

CHAPTER 8
How To Get Started

SO WHAT IS MEDITATION, and how do you start? Meditation is the act of controlling your own mind; not an easy task when you realize you've spent a lifetime letting it run its own course.

Every thought we have is an electrical signal traveling along our neural pathways, the system of roadways through which communication takes place in our brain. The more repetitive the thought, the stronger we make the pathway along which it runs. And the stronger the pathway is, the more often that thought will run itself (7). Look at the Grand Canyon. What started as a trickling stream created a huge chasm through which the Colorado River now flows.

Our brain has been running the show since we evolved and has helped us survive, but now we're living in a much safer world and we need to take control of our brains and mould it into something that feels more suitable to today's realities.

Are you ready for something new? I hope you're fist-pumping the air with excitement right now! The definition of insanity, as per a quote widely attributed to Albert Einstein, is repeating the same behaviour and expecting different results. Make today the day you do something different, something that will give you the results you're looking for – a life filled with a ton of love and peace you'll share with someone special.

I often tell people the first step to meditation is committing to it, and the best way to do this is to create some form of accountability. When I first imitated the Harvard meditation study I put a hand drawn chart on my fridge with eight rows and seven columns representing eight weeks. Every day I'd write the number of minutes I meditated, and when I reached the end of the week I'd calculate the average to make sure I was staying on track. Sure I missed a day here and there. Christmas and New Years were happening during my first eight weeks, and I had some busy or recuperative days, but I made those up by meditating more on other days. For me, the important part was averaging 27 minutes a day.

Did it help? Tremendously. I felt clear, and the business planning keeping me busy wasn't even a challenge. I started sleeping better, falling asleep earlier and sleeping more soundly. I started having moments where instead of being in freak-out mode I observed how calm I felt. I convinced my husband to make meditation a daily practice when he confessed how overwhelmed and stressed he felt from work; then watched him go from sleepless nights on the couch to sleeping through every night in bed as he became more calm and less stressed. I've witnessed many friends and clients change their lives and emotions through meditation, achieving fulfillment, happiness, and balance. I'm a firm believer now in the power of meditation, and I make meditation my go-to anxiety reducer because I can't imagine a life without this stress-busting habit.

Remember, unless you make time to love yourself every day it's unreasonable to expect the deeply loving relationship you're looking for. You get what you're ready and willing to receive, and meditation is the antennae through which you'll attract true love and commitment, because you send out the signal you yourself are committed to love.

Now, first go find the spots that will be your go-to for sitting uninterrupted during your sessions. This could be a variety of places: your office at home or at work, your bedroom, anywhere in your house or outside that can be private. If you live with people make them aware of what you're doing so you can get their co-operation for privacy.

You might think, *I don't have time for this! I rush around in the morning, spend the day rushing around at work, come home and make dinner, clean up, and whew! Thank God I have time to sit and watch TV for a bit.* Well, guess what? There's your time. Tell people, "I'm going to meditate for a bit," go into another room, listen to your favourite track, and take a moment to train your brain to become something that will serve you better. And don't underestimate the ripple effect you'll have, because once your loved ones see the change in you (and the goodness you attract into your life), they'll want to get on board too.

If you think there isn't enough time in the day to meditate, consider the Zen saying: "You should sit in meditation for 20 minutes a day, unless you're too busy; then you should sit for an hour." Basically, the crazier your life is, the more you need meditation to help navigate it. My new personal motto has become: Whatever I'm facing in life, meditate first.

So, you've put your chart up on the fridge, you have a sweet sitting spot picked out, and you've chosen music or guided meditations to help you along. Now what? Now you learn to quiet the monkeys in your head. Remember I mentioned how your brain is a network of neural pathways, with reinforced channels created by your own set of repetitive thoughts? Now is the time to create new pathways, in essence your new brain, by re-directing your thoughts to nothing. No words, no images, no random song weaving through your mind on repeat, no checklist of things to do. It's this concentrated focus on directing your own thoughts that will change the physical make-up of your brain.

When I was 25 I visited a yoga center near my apartment in a funky, creative area of downtown Montreal known as The Plateau. This Zen studio hosted monthly speakers teaching us meditation and yoga techniques, and on my first night I learned to imagine my thoughts as monkeys chattering and swinging in the trees, with our goal being to calm and quiet the monkeys. This analogy made it easier for me to identify and calm my own mental babble.

You may feel like quieting your mind is as easy as catching a greased piglet at first, which is completely normal because like any new undertaking this one will take practice to perfect. The fact is I've been meditating since I was 24, and even though I've made it a point to change my periodic practice into a (almost) daily habit, I still have to catch and quiet the monkeys in my tree. The important part is that you are, and you'll find with each session it'll get easier to bring your mind back under your control instead of watching it swing wildly where it chooses.

Breathe deeply and try to increase relaxation with each breath. Focus on your body and release any tension with every exhale. Make being in the present moment the goal you're reaching for. Bring your focus to the space   between your eyes or right in front of your face, breathe in and out of that space, and return there each time you find you've strayed into a thought. See your thoughts as tidbits of energy; every one you have beyond the present moment, whether it's compiling a grocery list or something you want to say later, is a piece of your energy flying away from you. Bring all your energy back to yourself by bringing your thoughts back to your present space, your present breath, and your present sensations.

Make this a moment where you can experience for yourself what having all your energy feels like. Enjoy it. Remind yourself that whatever is waiting for you in this world can wait 5, or 10, or 27 minutes, and know that nothing will fall apart in the meantime. Do this for as long as you can or until your meditation time is up, then go write your minutes on your chart and be proud of yourself for taking time to love you today.

If you're just starting to meditate and don't know what to listen to, find my YouTube channel. I have a playlist for you called "Let's Meditate" with a ton of great tracks you can use. I always recommend people start with the ten minute love frequency and then go from there. If you dedicate yourself to meditating to this track at least once a day I can promise you, your life will change. Be sure to send me an email letting me know how it's going for you. I love to hear your stories.

CHAPTER 9
I Know You've Heard This Before…
Like Attracts Like

WHY DO I SPEND SO MUCH TIME talking about meditation? Because I know you want to be in a happy relationship with a happy partner. I know you want to share the rest of your life with someone who lifts you up instead of drag you down. I want you to understand that your emotional state has everything to do with the sort of person you'll attract, and by starting with your own vibe you'll draw in those who'll increase your positive energy by melding it with their own. If you stay in a negative state that's exactly what you'll attract, and ultimately that's what you'll magnify in yourself and your relationships.

When you lift yourself up first, relationships become a cycle of lifting each other up even higher, and isn't that what true love is all about? Helping each other grow and rise to amazing levels of emotional rewards? By starting with your own frequency you'll attract someone as intent as you are in decoding what a loving union is all about.

I've been blessed with a deep gift of intuition, thanks to a natural talent that was expanded when my mind was opened to our ability to engage with other people's energy. It was my awakened intuition that told me my husband was the most beautiful person I'd ever met, and it was because of this inner knowledge that I struggled and fought my way through almost 10 years of unpacking emotional baggage together. But I knew once it was all unpacked, and it was just us, that what we shared would be nothing short of magical. And do you know what? It really is. It's as good as you can imagine a relationship being, filled with love, kindness, and consideration. I understood early on he was the doorway to all this amazingness, but it took me 9 years to understand meditation was the key to unlocking it.

The love I receive every day from my husband is amazing. What I want for you is to experience this amazingness because I know you can. Everyone can. It's a gift just waiting to be picked up, and the fact is you're already holding the gift card in your hand. All it takes is a trip to the store to collect it and, lucky for you, the store is right inside your head, open 24/7. Love is already inside of you, the deepest most fulfilling love you've ever experienced. Accept it, feel it, exude it, and attract it. Click your ruby red shoes together and come home now.

STEP 2
Clarity

Your mind is like the antennae in your phone, constantly sending a signal that's being picked up by like minds. Clarify what you want, know what you don't want, and that signal will start to deliver a whole new caliber of people to your life.

CHAPTER 10
Help!

UGH, I CAN'T HANDLE THIS! I thought, staring at the piles of paper littering my coffee table. It was a month into the birth of my career in Human Relations, and I was busy taking my knowledge and rolling it into a new business. I could feel the ideas jamming in my mind like too many boulders trying to make their way through a funnel, and the strain of trying to sort them out was frustrating me.

I huffed a moment longer, then surrendered and grabbed my iPad. Maybe taking my mind off my brain for a bit would help.

I flipped through social media for a few minutes and came across a headline, "Eight Weeks to a Better Brain." *What a coincidence*, I thought, *I was just thinking I needed a new brain.*

I started meditating daily and within a week felt the ideas start to flow again, leading to even greater visions of where my business could go. Suddenly, it was time to truly conceptualize what I wanted from this life.

I made my first vision board on a large piece of construction paper and filled it with images of women giving talks to large audiences, surrounded with powerful words like *made something better* and *I take pleasure in my transformations.*

    I bought a cork board and began laying out my first seminar. As the ideas gushed out I wrote furiously, developing them into simple steps that would ultimately populate my first workbook. Suddenly, I was well on my way to not only giving birth to seminars, but to my first published book. I felt clearer every day, and the faith I began to develop within myself brought me to tears at times. Life had opened up, and I thanked my commitment to clarity for the golden opportunities I saw on the road ahead of me.

CHAPTER 11
Know Thyself

HOW COMFORTABLE WOULD YOU BE, travelling to a new destination with only a vague address and no map? If somebody proposed doing this you'd probably call them nuts, but it's exactly what happens when you're looking for the "perfect partner" without clarifying who he is first. A lot of people think, *I'll know when I meet him*, but if your intuition has been off base so far what makes you think it'll be spot- on the next time around? If you're blindly throwing darts chances are you'll keep missing the bulls-eye, and only pure luck will help you nail it.

But luck doesn't have to be the only thing in your favour. You can increase your odds of finding a great man by delving deep into yourself and figuring out what works for you. As much as meditation helps you unlock the door to your intuition and the answers deep within, clarity helps you crystalize the your knowledge of what you deserve in a relationship and break the pattern of what you've been getting.

But before you even step on the road to an everlasting relationship, you need to know what makes you feel loved. I mean, reeeeaaaalllly figure out what makes you feel loved, not what you think makes you feel loved. There's a book called

The Five Love Languages by Gary Chapman (1). Through his practice as a relationship counselor Gary realized we display and perceive love in five different ways:

- Physical Touch, where we express our love and commitment through affection like cuddling, holding hands, and kissing

- Gifts, when we find joy in giving and receiving presents in tune with what we want and need

- Acts of Service, my husband's big one, where you express and feel love through willingness to help any time it's needed, like shoveling snow or moving furniture

- Quality Time, for those who need to know their presence is the most desirable thing in the world

- Words of Affirmation, where hearing what amazing qualities your partner sees fill you with certainty you're loved and cherished.

By seeing these five loving qualities as separate languages we can understand how lines can get crossed in relationships, and avoid pitfalls caused by miscommunications.

Think of it this way: if I spoke to you in French but all you've ever spoken is German, you're not going to understand a word I say. But if I know you only speak German and I take the time to learn your language, I can interpret what you say and make an effort to communicate with you in a way you'll understand.

For example, when my husband and I took the Love Language Quiz we both had two languages emerge as equally dominant. For me it was Physical Touch and Words of Affirmation, while his turned out to be Physical Touch and Acts of Service. So while we were perfectly matched on our desire to share love through Physical Touch, we were suffering because we didn't understand the mistakes we were making in our partner's other, equally important Love Language. All this was compounded by the fact we didn't get to see each other as much as we would have liked. He worked from early morning until late at night, and I worked night shifts. The time we got to spend together amounted to about 10 hours a week. Not much time for cuddling.

My husband is also what you'd call a man's man, with few words to spare. So it's no surprise that within the first year I started to feel an emptiness in my love bank. Little time to snuggle and almost no words of affirmation left me feeling unloved, and I said so to him.

"What?!" he said with outraged indignation each time I brought it up. "I cleaned your basement when it flooded! And I helped you take a door down and moved your stove and…" He'd list all the things he'd done to show he loved me, but I didn't get it. While it was great he did all those man things around the house, I needed to hear he appreciated me and that I was precious to him.

Lucky for us, we took the Love Language quiz and figured out our mistakes. For a while after that I still had moments where I felt unloved (old habits die hard), but I'd stop myself and think, *Okay, you're feeling unloved, but what has he done for you lately?* I'd go through my memory and find all of those big and little things he'd been doing to help me and tell myself those were the love signals I'd been missing.

In essence, I would interpret his actions and see clearly that he did in fact love me, filling myself up on his acts of service instead of words. By doing this exercise I taught myself it was okay to not get all the words I needed from him alone and learned to appreciate the ones I received from friends and family more.

By being open and balanced in my needs I was able to create more peace and relaxation in my relationship, and my man was grateful I wasn't handing over 100% of the responsibility for helping me feel loved. I also became a yes woman whenever he asked me for a favour, recognizing that any other answer would leave him feeling unloved and unappreciated.

It's important to know your love language and have a clear idea which one is vital to you. While I would never compromise and give up physical touch in a relationship, being aware that words of affirmation also matter gives me insight on how I can distribute my love languages, keeping my romantic relationship free from undue strain.

Knowing how you feel loved also offers insight into what sort of partner you should look for, and helps you teach your partner how he can accomplish loving you when you speak different languages. And gaining insight into his love language helps avoid unnecessary fights because you have a greater understanding on what makes his heart tick. The more you understand love, the better it can flow throughout your life.

CHAPTER 12
Know Your Value

LET'S BE CLEAR ON WHAT'S VALUABLE about you as a person. Until we see in black and white just what makes us special, it can be hard to stand up for what we deserve. There's nothing egotistical in simply acknowledging your own traits, and being able to say hello to all your positive qualities can be a boost to your confidence. Unlock your inner beauty so it can shine for the entire world to see. Tap into what people like about you and revel in it. Really bask in the appreciation you get because of who you are and what you contribute.

Make friends with what makes you unique and amazing. Be prepared to give yourself the standing ovation of your life because unless you can acknowledge your qualities, your femininity, your intelligence, your humour, your helpful nature, your ability to think and plan, anything and everything that's a strength within you, you'll never be prepared to allow someone else to love you just the way you are. Give yourself permission to acknowledge yourself and flourish under your own love; it's the only way you'll be prepared to blossom under the loving gaze of another human being.

So grab a piece of paper and a pen and write at the top, "I Am," and start writing out everything good about you. Don't stop until there are no more I am statements you can think of, or reach a minimum of 50 statements. Keep it positive, because this is the moment to learn to acknowledge your positive attributes and to push aside any negative self- talk. Are you organized? Then write, "I am organized." How about a sharp dresser? "I am stylish." Do you like the curve of your hips and how they swing when you walk? "I am sexy." Do you make people comfortable around you? "I am considerate." Don't be afraid to give each and every positive attribute its own statement.

I felt increasingly empowered as I wrote my own list. When I was finished it was like I was finally seeing who I was, and I felt proud of myself. I knew then and there that I was a catch and that only a great man would find his way into my heart, because I recognized that I was a woman worthy of someone amazing.

Next, take another piece of paper and write, "3 Reasons why a man would LOVE to be with me." If you can think up more than three, great! But if you struggle to find three don't stop this exercise until you do. If you can't find three reasons why you're an awesome person to be with, you risk entering a relationship not knowing the qualities you bring and are in danger of being walked on and hurt. I'll help you with one right now: "A man would love to be with me because my thirst for knowledge and self-improvement keeps me seeking answers and finding inspiration in the world around me."

Knowing your power and standing firmly in it helps make you a whole person, and bringing wholeness to your next relationship is an important factor for making it work.

Knowing your qualities helps you understand what's important for you and clarifies what sort of man you want to be with, because at the end of the day we're most comfortable with what feels familiar and a vital key to moving towards a better relationship is having perspective on who you are. Know thyself, in all your glorious qualities, and watch as incredible men are drawn to your light like a moth to a flame.

Chapter 13

What Do I Want?

THIS IS THE SINGLE MOST IMPORTANT QUESTION you can ask yourself. Ever. If you can't answer this there's no way anyone can make you happy, because you'll only have a vague idea about what self-fulfillment actually means to you. The most unfair thing you can ask of someone else is to make you happy when you don't even know what that entails. You need to understand what will give you satisfaction and go out seeking it instead of demanding anyone in your life try to figure it out for you.

The What Do I Want? exercise can be applied to any area of your life. Contemplating a change in careers and feeling uncertain? Not sure whether to downsize or upsize your home? Start your journey with "What do I want?" Life can be confusing when there're so many options to consider, but boiling it down to what your heart is saying helps guide you in the right direction. So let's do this now to identify your ideal partner.

Grab a piece of paper and write, "What do I want in My Ideal Partner" at the top and start writing every quality you desire in your next man. Generous? Kind? Loves animals?

Sensual? Has a sense of humour? Affectionate? Works out? Can chop down a tree? Goes for walks? Is sociable? Likes movies or just generally getting out of the house? Is a homebody? Has children or would accept yours? What's important to you? List them ALL.

Now, think about your past relationships. What did you enjoy about them? What qualities would you like to see repeated in your next relationship? Enjoys dancing? Thinks farts are funny? List them. Then reflect on what you didn't like about your exes and put the opposite down. Was he rude to waiters? Write, "Is patient and kind to people." Did he yell when you had fights? Write, "Has good conflict resolution tools." Fill this paper up, no detail is too big or small.

Now, get specific. I know you wrote, "Is considerate" on there. Ask yourself, considerate how? To strangers? Wait staff? Dogs? How does he exhibit this trait? Brings you coffee in the morning? If you wrote, "Is fit", write what sort of workout you'd like to share with him. Are you okay if he has kids? Write down what age limit you're willing to take on. Really examine your life and what would fit best.

When you can't think of anything more, put this list where you'll see it every day. On your desk or fridge is the ideal spot, and keep a pen handy too. You're going to think of more things to add as you have conversations with friends or see something on TV that creates a yearning. Add those to the list. You can't make this list too long. The more detailed you are the better you understand what you want for yourself, and the clearer your wants are the better you'll be able to recognize the man you're looking for when he's standing in front of you.

Remember, you're an antennae sending out a signal; the biggest mistake you can make is to send the wrong signal for who should come into your life.

CHAPTER 14
Clearly Attracting That Perfect Man

NOW, I KEEP SAYING THIS but it's sooooo important to understand —like attracts like. Look at your list again. This man is pursuing someone like him because we seek what's familiar. Is there anything on this list that doesn't embody who you are? If yes, then you have something you can work on.

If you listed *loves to go for walks* because you're looking for someone to encourage you to get walking, that's not fair. Unless you create this habit before meeting him, it's possible that even his influence won't get you outside. Make this part of your life now, and when you meet up it's simply a matter of joining each other on your walks. How romantic!

Change is not a bad thing by the way. You need to evolve past who you are to find who you want, because if you haven't met Mr. Right already it's possible you don't embody the familiar feeling (or signal) your ideal man is seeking. Yet.

Embrace growth; it's a beautiful thing that brings all you want in life. Tweak yourself, and attract the man you're dreaming of. Did you write on your list *is patient* but you have a short temper? Then this patient man will eventually grow tired of your short fuse, so work on becoming a more Zen person through regular meditation.

Become similar to the man you seek, and you'll attract him much faster, because he'll recognize a like energy when he meets you and fall head over heels for all your familiar qualities.

CHAPTER 15
No More

NOW THAT YOU'RE GETTING CLEAR on what you do and don't want in your next relationship, you need to go one step further and keep the bullshit that tainted your last relationships from rearing its ugly head again. This is the most powerful part of your Clarity. It's called the No More exercise, and unless you do it, and can do it with conviction, you'll keep getting dragged into the same drama that made you unhappy in your past relationships.

Here's how this came about for me.

I had a pattern to my boyfriends; they tended to be the sort of guys who were controlling and/or insecure, and we constantly fought over these issues. Jeff was physically abusive, Luis didn't give me the time of day unless I paid his way, Derick was trying to woo one of his college friends and using me to make her jealous, and Roger was having secret relationships with girls he met after we started dating.

Finally, I'd had enough. I mean, I'd *really* had enough. Something rose up inside me, a strength and conviction that I'd never felt before, and I had my No More moment right there in my kitchen.

I'd met Roger, my final disastrous relationship, while on a rock climbing road trip with a girlfriend. He liked my sarcastic humour, I was attracted to his outgoing personality, and the chemistry between us created major sparks. It wasn't long before we were an item, and at his coaxing I picked up and moved from Montreal to his picturesque city near Toronto. And then reality set in.

It quickly became clear that Roger needed female attention... a lot of it. He made new friends everywhere he went, but none of them were male. He'd rush to the computer first thing every morning to message his new female friends before heading to school, and when he came home he'd jump back online to chat until bedtime. Any time I questioned his motives he'd accuse me of being blind to the purity of his heart, but any male friends I had were given a scathing review as guys were just after one thing.

The fights became too much and we broke up, but stayed roommates and found a comfort zone in a friends with benefits arrangement. He was leaving soon to pursue a career opportunity in Colorado, and with the pressures of a committed relationship off the table we had more peace between us. Despite our problems my immature mind hoped he'd ask me to move with him, but after some back and forth he kyboshed the notion, and I committed myself to staying in Ontario.

He left for Colorado and I began my new, single life. I started to become social again, and when Roger called me out of the blue one day I mentioned I was on my way out with a new friend, a guy named Mike. Next thing I knew the calls from Roger became more frequent, we started fighting again, and then he tossed out this statement:

"I was planning on asking you to move here and be with me."

I lost it.

"That's not fair!" I yelled, and hung up on him.

Suddenly, I could see through his manipulations and understood what he really wanted wasn't *me*, but to keep me under his thumb and control my attention. He hated the thought of losing my focus to someone else and didn't give a crap about my own happiness. His self-interest trumped all.

"No more assholes!!" I yelled up at the ceiling of my basement apartment, arms raised in surrender. I said it with force, I said it with conviction, and I said it with every fiber of my being. I felt that message come up from the innermost depths of my soul and vibrate through my body, and something left me that moment. It was the part of me that accepted being part of someone else's constant drama. It was the part of me that bowed down and tolerated anything just to be with someone I thought I loved. It was the part of me that thought it was okay if love was a prison. I felt all that rise out of me, and I became lighter, more certain about myself, and happier about where my life was going. I was done with assholes, and I knew it.

What about you? What's your pattern? Maybe you don't have a history of being with insecure jerks, but you have a habit of attracting men who don't have time to spend with you (No more being unimportant!) or who can't hold a job (No more irresponsible guys!). One lady at my last seminar had an issue with guys who were always late, so hers was No more disrespecting my time!

So what's your No More statement? Write it down and take a moment to vibrate this new personal truth. Until you do, you won't be done attracting the same thing over and over.

Closing the door on what was dysfunctional in your past relationships opens the door for true, functioning love to come through. Don't block yourself from being loved by someone who'll truly care for you, just because you haven't changed the subconscious message you don't deserve better than the crap you've been putting up with. Love doesn't have to require a sacrifice of your inner peace. Now is the time to learn to just say "No!" when the next guy comes around offering the same poo on a platter.

STEP 3

Overcoming Fear

Fear can be your biggest obstacle when it comes to achieving true love. Recognize where it holds you back and step through into something new.

CHAPTER 16
Nothing Wrong With Change

"WANT TO COME TO A PARTY?" asked my downstairs neighbor.

"Okay!" I said before the sudden fear that leaped into my throat could strangle my words. Previous experiences at parties, specifically those where the only person I knew was the one who brought me, were not good. It's wasn't that I couldn't talk to people, but starting conversations felt near impossible. I'd stand around trying to look cool despite every part of my body exhibiting classic social anxiety symptoms. There I'd be, palms sweating, stomach twisted and tied in knots, my mouth a dry cottony mess, shaking like a leaf and desperately hoping some kind soul would come say "hi." I knew I had a problem.

When my neighbor invited me to the party I instantly realized I had an opportunity to tackle my fear. I was tired of feeling helpless, unable to do what I truly wanted: talk to anybody and everybody. I craved more social contact, but fear was pushing me into corners and up against walls.

Nobody knew me, I told myself. I would go with the kind of pristine record that only comes with lack of history.   No one had a clue I was nervous when it came to social situations, that

I was still building my self-esteem, that I had a track record of being a painfully shy wallflower whenever I went to a party and was forced to fend for myself.

Nobody. Not even my neighbor. I could make a different impression this time; I could create a new version of me.

With the party coming up in two weeks, I decided to prepare. I bought a book *How to Work a Room* by Susan RoAne and devoured it. Susan instructed me to read the newspaper the day before and have opinions on world events. She told me to not tie myself to just one person, but mingle and remember that I always had something in common with other people; namely, what brought us together.

Watch your body language, directed Susan. Lucky for me I'd dated someone who'd been a master at affecting body language, and I had studied his easy way of communicating with people. I drew on memories of how he carried himself, the way he held eye contact, kept his shoulders back, and telegraphed confidence in every movement.

And then the big day came. I stood before the door with my neighbor, trying to swallow past the lump in my throat, feeling as anxious and nervous as ever. Staring at that door was like looking at my literal door to change, and I said to myself, *I WILL be different.* I knew in that moment I was about to step into the unknown and shift my entire life.

"Hey! Come on in!" said the host as he opened the door, inviting us inside his cozy apartment. He took a moment to chat, but soon I found myself alone while my neighbor gravitated towards friends and my host drifted away to see to his guests.

This is it, I said to myself, and with a huge mental push made my way to the food table. "How do you know the host?" I asked one of the girls, hoping she wouldn't notice my shaking hands while I forced down some chips. We talked for a half hour before I reminded myself that practice makes perfect; it was time to push beyond my comfort zone again and repeat the process.

"How do you know the host?" I asked a guy in the kitchen beside the drinks counter, ignoring the pounding of my heart. Forty-five minutes later I warned myself once again to not get tied down to just one person. I excused myself and looked for another lonely soul.

"Hi, I'm Chantal," I said with a smile. "How do you know the host?"

Before the night ended I was invited to another party. I practiced more at that one and found myself invited to the next, where a girl invited me to her own upcoming get together. "Yes, I'd love to!" I said, feeling like I was being gifted with opportunities to polish my new skills.

And then it happened.

It was at this fourth party that I went from Faking It to Making It.

"You're so self-assured!" said one of the girls who'd been at the last party. "I wish I could be more like you!"

My confidence instantly skyrocketed, and suddenly I felt completely confident and truly, sincerely, self-assured. Her acknowledgement of my behaviours had a profound effect; it cemented my new social powers into my psyche. In that moment I graduated from someone trying to be more confident to someone who simply was, and still is, more confident.

I'd learned how to work past my brain and create an illusion, but the magic of it all materialized; I was no longer that wallflower. I'd become a new person, able to walk into any room and confidently own my space. I'd decided who I wanted to be and had behaved my way to success.

I'm not saying I never feel fear anymore, because I do. But I have confidence in my ability to behave in a way that matches my goals instead of bowing to feelings of fear about approaching people who can help make my dreams come true. I've decided to be courageous, and in the process I have removed my obstacles.

CHAPTER 17

Fear Not

WHAT IS FEAR? Doubt, anxiety, dread, unease, panic. When you boil it down to its basic premise it's simply a feeling, and unless you find yourself in a scene from a horror movie it's not reality. Fear, when you're looking at someone and afraid to approach, is just a feeling. Fear, when you're faced with a decision to either lower your standards or be alone, is just a feeling. And it's the worst kind of feeling, because it can come between you and what you truly want and deserve.

It's what happens when you ask your brain, "Should I do this?" and the answer is, "Wait, we've never done that before!" or "Well, you know the last time we did this it sucked." It's a reaction in your body to the unknown, or to the perceived danger you face day in and day out. The part of your brain that generates fear is interested in nothing but self-preservation, but because its tentacles reach far and wide fear can be your biggest stumbling block when it comes to attracting the man who's right for you.

But what if you didn't feel fear? Or what if you had enough courage to face fear and do it anyway? You can, you just need to have the right tools. Fortunately for you, you're already wearing the tool belt, and it's just a matter of putting that hammer in your hand. There's nothing wrong with overriding fear any way you can, but you're on the wrong track if you think you should let it direct what you do in life.

CHAPTER 18

Fake It
(No One Will Ever Know)

"FAKE IT 'TIL YOU MAKE IT. Oh my God that's such a cliché!" I hear some people say, but there's a reason this statement has withstood the test of time: It works because it calls on the principle of practicing your butt off. Were you a pro at horseback riding or Excel spreadsheets or salsa dancing when you decided to learn? No, but when you did it for the first time you stepped on the same path as the professional who'd already done it a thousand.

Overcoming fear is the perfect next step after opening your intuition through meditation and clarifying what you want. Without this step your capabilities are frozen when you see the man who makes your heart skip a beat.

Understand that your body is your number one communication tool, both inward to yourself and out to the world. Knowing how communication happens between the body and the brain can be the most important thing you'll ever learn. With 93% of our communications being non- verbal, 55% through body language alone and 38% through tone of voice (1), it's important to be aware of the message you're sending to people and your own mind.

To your mind? Yes! Believe it or not, you are the biggest influence on how you think and feel, and unless you know this and control the message you're just along for the ride. Take those little muscles that crinkle around your eyes when you smile and laugh. They contract when your brain triggers your dopamine neurotransmitter and signals that something amusing or happy just happened. But it works in reverse too; if you initiate a big smile, those muscles tell your brain something fun just happened and your brain in turn will release dopamine (2), delivering a dose of happy feelings. And just seeing someone smile creates a dopamine release, which is why a smile is the first thing you want to give when looking to attract the man across the room.

By the way, this is the reason I stopped getting Botox injections around my eyes—when I found out those muscles were broadcasters of happiness to my brain my first reaction was to wonder if freezing them was the reason I'd been feeling blue. So I gave up on Botox and made peace with my laugh lines, just in case. Men would rather not be with a sad woman, no matter how wrinkle-free her face is. In fact, they're geared to seek happiness on our faces... but more on that later.

The justice system is aware of the connection between your body and your brain too. When interrogators question a suspect they do so with a keen eye on body language, because the truth will usually come from fidgeting hands or pursed lips instead of the words coming out of their mouths. *Micro expressions* is the term they use to describe that split second reaction when what happens in the mind is involuntarily telegraphed on the face.

What about you? Are you confident? If you have trouble starting a conversation and the thought of flirting with a man makes your palms sweat, there's hope; you can trick yourself into feeling confident by using your body to create courage from the outside in.

Amy Cuddy gives an amazing Ted Talk on power poses, ways to re-arrange your body and trick your brain. The fact is, don't have to be a prisoner of your own assumptions. You can change who you are by using behaviour and leading your brain down the path you actually want to travel, rather than surrendering to where you are right now and accepting this as the status quo.

For example, say you want to flirt with the cute man you always see at the coffee shop. You can sit at home and worry yourself to death about how nervous you are, or you can decide to increase your confidence by doing a simple exercise. First, let's think about the worrying body language: Your shoulders are slumped forward, your chin is low, and you're likely not smiling. The message to your brain is, I am in a self-protective and unhappy mode.

But what if you said to yourself *I'm going to do this like a champ!* What does a champion do when they cross that finish line? Their arms shoot up in victory, their chests puff out full of pride, and they have the biggest smiles you've ever seen on their faces. Their brains can't help releasing a huge amount of dopamine and testosterone.

Instead of stressing about how approaching the cute man will go and expecting to feel disappointed in your execution, you can reverse the flow of emotions. By essentially doing a victory dance before your approach you can increase the dopamine in your brain to boost your happiness, raising the amount of pep you put into your approach and intensifying the pleasure that attractive man will have when you talk to him. This increases the likelihood of him responding favourably, boosting your self-esteem and confidence. And the next time you approach a cute man those feelings will linger, feeding your mind and helping you flirt with even more confidence. So hit the bathroom, raise your arms over your head and have a "Rah-Rah!" moment to boost your dopamine. Or play rocking girl power music every day and have a dance off in your living room. Arms up, baby! Celebrate yourself and what you want from life!

Personally, I'm frequently adjusting my body language because we can easily fall into a trap of subconsciously pulling ourselves down. Shoulders back and relaxed, spine straight, heart out, chin up. All these little steps help me go about my day feeling more confident, and it telegraphs my confidence to people. You've heard the saying you can't demand respect, but you can command it? By showing people in a non-verbal way you love yourself you send a signal to their brain that they subconsciously respond to. Show the world you're fearless, and it will treat you as a warrior. With

time and practice, being courageous will become second
nature to you, and not even the fluttering in your belly will get
between you and the love you're seeking.

It takes a lot of courage to master love, and if you don't
practice before finding the perfect man your fear could drive
him right out of your life. I've scared away my share of
amazing prospects because I let fear turn me into a freakazoid.
It was only after I made peace with the fear in my belly and
taught myself to move forward despite it that I finally found
the love I'd been looking for.

CHAPTER 19
What is Fear?

BACK WHEN WE WERE LIVING IN CAVES fear was our greatest ally. It taught us what we should stay away from and kept us from exploring things that were threats to our lives, like venomous snakes or treacherous cliffs.

I studied the fundamentals of fear when I became a dog trainer and behaviour modification specialist over 20 years ago and used that knowledge to explain bad behaviour and helpful training techniques to owners. I learned early on that fear is something that creeps up on all of us, and the less we practice bravely facing new scenarios the harder it becomes as we age. Why are we all like this? By turning to wolf psychology, I found the answer.

When wolf pups are born they spend the first few weeks developing their sight and hearing, but once that happens they start exploring in earnest. Their sense of fear is almost non-existent but their size and mobility means they're not going far anyway. This gives them the freedom to explore their surroundings with confidence under the watchful eye of the wolf pack who keep their environment free from danger, much like your parents did for you when you were a toddler. But as they grow and become more mobile they explore further away, and at this stage their fear response starts to kick in. Since they're wandering beyond the safety of the den anything they encounter poses a potential threat, and their fear keeps them from getting too close to lethal dangers.

It's the same thing with us. We now have a fear response to what's new and unfamiliar, but that doesn't necessarily mean that what strikes fear into our hearts is worth being afraid of. It could just be our minds saying, *This is outside of my past experiences, and therefore outside my comfort zone.* Think about every time you stopped yourself from doing something out of fear. How many times has it kept you from maintaining eye contact with a man who made your heart speed up? Could this be why you're not in his arms right now?

We have a lot of what we call common fears today, but if we're smart we won't let them bog us down and hold us hostage. Fear of being alone, fear of looking stupid, fear of failure, of change, of pain, rejection, commitment, abandonment, of being taken advantage of, and the most common one, fear of the unknown, are all just fears of things that haven't happened yet. Don't let them run your life and you'll have more experiences to feel satisfied about, like walking down the street holding hands with someone who truly cares about you.

CHAPTER 20
Practice Makes Perfect

ANOTHER CLICHÉ, I KNOW… but there's truth to it. The more your body sends positive messages to your brain, the more your brain's plasticity will take those messages and form them into reality. This is what I love about our minds: We are only as trapped as we think we are, and the moment we decide to shake free of our shackles we can step out of them and into a new reality. It doesn't happen overnight, but with persistence and dedication you can behave your way to a new way of being and feeling.

I want you to imagine the last time fear stopped you from getting to know a man or held you back from going over and talking to him. Really put yourself in that moment and feel those butterflies wildly dancing around in your stomach. Close your eyes and imagine all the physiological responses you go through. Is your heart in your throat? Are your hands shaking a bit? Is your stomach in a knot?

Now I want you to imagine using these seven techniques to override the feelings that stop you dead in your tracks. Use your imagination and see yourself going through each step, right here and now, and monitor what changes happen inside of you.

1) **Breathe.** Three deep, slow breaths will cut your anxiety and stress while increasing your sense of inner peace and relaxation. So before you do anything, take a moment to take threeeeee deeeeeeep, sloooooooow breaths.

2) **Watch your body language.** It's hard to feel confident when your body is screaming, *I just want to hide!* Pay attention to the message your body is giving and change it to convey what you really want to communicate. Remember, work that information outside in. Practice your power poses. Standing with your hands on your hips or leaning back in your chair with your hands on the armrests are great, open body languages. Avoid crossed arms or legs; these close you up and send the signal you're feeling helpless and defensive. Smile big! It signals your brain you're in a good place, releasing a rush of dopamine that will help elevate your mood and confidence.

3) **Relax.** Relax those tight shoulders, that clenched fist, your knotted stomach and clenched jaw. Loosen up. Use your three deep breaths to release tension on each exhale.

4) **Be prepared.** Knowing your stuff is vital to being confident in what you do, so prepare, prepare, prepare. If you're giving a presentation, practice it on a friend or family member first. The first time doing anything can be the hardest and most nerve wracking, so get that out of the way. Consider the first few times you approach a

man your practice runs, and don't be attached to the outcome. Imagine yourself going through a scenario from beginning to end and being a rock star in the process. Imagine how happy and confident you'll feel after a winning episode.

5) **Be curious.** If you're going to a social gathering, read up on current events and have opinions on what's going on in the world; these will be your talking points. Ask a lot of questions when you have a conversation; this helps break the ice and eases the pressure of coming up with stuff to say. Visualize yourself engrossed in conversation with someone you really want to hit a home run with and see his eyes taking you in with interest and appreciation.

6) **Fake it.** If you're feeling fearful, that's okay. If you behave as though you're not afraid, then your fear will be temporary, and no one will ever know you were a hot mess inside. Fear is like a monster with an insatiable appetite; the more you feed it the bigger it gets. Don't give it the time of day, and it'll starve itself out. Envision yourself appearing cool as a cucumber on the outside, impressing those around you with your social skills and ability to put them at ease. Feel their gratitude because they're happy they could just relax around you.

7) **Do it anyway.** That's right, just do it. Fear doesn't have to stop you, it doesn't have to control you, and it doesn't have to be anything more than a sensation in

your stomach. Acknowledge it and then go out and conquer life. Great things happen on the other side of fear, because fear is just your brain's way of saying, Beware! Uncharted territory! Life and love await your ready heart, so realize you can master whatever comes your way because your courage and desires are greater than your fear.

CHAPTER 21

What Attracts the RIGHT Sort of Man

WHY IS CONFIDENCE SO KEY to attracting the right man? Because the #1 quality that gets a good man's attention is confidence. The man you're looking for is out there, metaphorically clubbing saber tooth tigers (or flesh-eating kangaroos. Can you imagine?) and bringing them home. He takes pride in his abilities to be a protector and provider, and he's subconsciously seeking a woman who has strength and pride too. He doesn't need her to be as physically strong, but seeing a woman with confidence triggers his lizard brain, telling him she's a worthy mate capable of surviving alongside him.

You want to avoid attracting the sort of guy who'll be happy you lack self-esteem and assurance. This is the one who'll walk all over you, take advantage of your fears and in the end leave you feeling used and lonely. There's nothing quite like confidence to act as a guy repellant. When you increase your confidence you instantly raise the bar, letting guys know you're not just going to pick whoever is paying attention to you while keeping yourself open for the man who'll appreciate the faith you have in yourself.

Just remember, fear is your reaction to the unknown. Confidence is the ability to act despite fear, and the more you practice behaving confidently, the easier it gets and the more life opens up and gives you exactly what you want. Whether it's a job opportunity or loving relationship, confidence is key to stepping into the growth required to get to the next level.

STEP 4
Connecting

We are human beings designed to connect with each other. Nothing makes our hearts pump harder, our bodies react stronger, and our minds race faster than the prospect of creating a romantic connection. Connecting is the first step in the intricate dance we share with each other, and once we master the steps we can tango with anyone we please.

CHAPTER 22
The Ride of My Life

"WHERE CAN I FIND BATTERIES for my video camera?" I asked the clerk at Sears.

"Fourth floor" she replied, pointing to a nearby escalator. I wandered over, not realizing I was about to embark on one of the most romantic stories I'd ever get to tell.

Stepping on the escalator at the first floor, I casually looked around as the smooth motion lulled me into a relaxed space. I glanced behind me and noticed two men, one of them incredibly tall and handsome. *Ooo,* I thought as my heart skipped, and I quickly turned around hoping he hadn't caught me doing a double take. At the top I rounded the corner and hopped on the next escalator, heading for the third floor.

Halfway up I looked back, not expecting to see the tall stranger, but there he was, looking straight up at me. My heart jumped up in my throat this time, and I felt my body jolt with a sudden thrill of electricity. I quickly turned around again, my face flushing fifty shades of red while my breath tried to jiggle its way past my heart, which suddenly seemed to have hijacked my body with its intense pounding.

Holy crap, I thought. He was hot. Like, I've-never-seen-such-a-gorgeous-man hot. Tall and broad shouldered, with sandy brown hair casually swept to the side and stylish glasses adding an air of sophistication to his rugged good looks and square jaw, his piercing eyes seemed to bore straight into me. His friend was a stark contrast, his slighter build accentuated by olive skin and jet black hair. He smiled slightly at me as our eyes met, amused at the girl staring at his tall companion.

Both time and the escalator slowed to crawl, and as I clutched the rail in a death grip I desperately hoped I wasn't telegraphing a furious blush through the back of my hair. *Oh shitshitshitshit!* I thought as my heart intensified its pounding in my chest, and all I could hear was the blood rushing through my ears.

At the third floor, feigning a casual grace I was positive nobody was being fooled by, I turned the corner and stepped onto the last escalator.

I looked around again, and there he was. In a moment of pure courage mingled with chutzpah, I smiled and flirtatiously blurted, "Are you following me?" I turned before he could answer, mortified at what had just come out of my mouth. I thought the red flush in my face would blow my head clean off my body, and I felt myself shaking like a leaf. *Ohmygod, ohmygod, ohmygod!* I kept saying in my head, occasionally reminding myself to breathe. Surely he could see right through my back, and the hot mess I'd turned into was so obvious the whole world would see.

Finally, I arrived at the fourth floor and, spotting the video section, set off to get my battery, thinking the whole, crazy ride was over.

I was wrong.

"Hi," I heard just a few steps into my walk. I stopped and turned as he walked over, a look of amusement playing across his face while his friend pretended to be interested in the shelves of radios beside him.

"What are you looking for?" he asked.

"A battery for my video camera," I replied, taking him in. Wow. What had seemed handsome from a distance was magnified as his kind, calm demeanor washed over me. I felt myself settle a bit, my heart still in my throat but not threatening to choke me any longer.

"Maybe I can help you?" We walked to the counter as he introduced himself. "I'm Charles," he said warmly.

I bought my battery while he hovered beside me, all 6'4" of him emanating a sweet, gentle energy that began to sooth my nerves. We chatted a moment. Where are you from? How long are you in town for? We were both visiting Vancouver, he from Seattle and I from Montreal, and we agreed to meet for supper that night at the city's classic revolving restaurant. Supper turned into a walk on the foggy beachfront, which turned into hot chocolate at a tiny hole in the wall cafe, and ended with a kiss at my hotel as I stood on a stair to reach his full, warm lips.

We stayed in touch and I travelled to his beautiful home nestled in the Seattle hillsides, turning our magical date into a long distance romance punctuated by horse drawn carriage rides and bedtime stories read over the phone. But eventually my intense wish to continue exploring the world pushed me on, and we said our goodbyes. It was an exciting time, and I'll never forget how my spontaneous and courageous acts sparked an unforgettable romantic journey with a tall, gorgeous, amazing man.

CHAPTER 23

Where Are All the Good MenAt?

LADIES, THEY ARE EVERYWHERE. Literally. So why is this the most common question? Why do women feel it's so hard to meet a great man? I have a few theories.

1) Maybe you're too shy. I mean, how do you know whether he's a good man if you never go up and talk to him? You could be surrounded by amazing men every time you step outside your house, but if he's thinking *she must be taken* and not coming up to you, you'll never find out if he's a potential fit unless you talk to him first.

2) Your intuition needs calibrating. The butterflies in your stomach and the flush in your cheeks should be your guide when it comes to zeroing in on a potential mate, but if you've been picking dead-weights in the past it could mean your inner voice isn't getting through properly.

3) You're not getting out there. You won't find a great man in your living room ("Scotty, beam me in a good one."), so unless you're hitting some social hot spots like coffee shops or manly habitats like sporting

events and auto shows, you're reducing your chances of running across the man of your dreams.

Here's the thing about men: Biologically speaking, they're geared to over-estimate when women are flirting with them. I'm sure you've had moments where you're being friendly, and next thing you know he's putting his hand on your waist and asking you to dinner. *Wait!* you think, *I was just being nice!* So you tell him as politely as you can that no, sorry, you're not interested in him. After a few rounds of being shot down men can sometimes become a little gun shy when it comes to leading the dating dance with women.

We used to make it so easy for men to understand what was going on in our minds. Back in Victorian times, courtship was triggered when a woman dropped her handkerchief in front of a man who caught her fancy. He in turn would pick it up and as he offered it back ask, "I'm sorry m'lady, but is this yours?" Game on. But what do we do today to let men know we'd like them to come calling? A wink on a dating website? A hopeful glance?

You need to be more obvious if you want him to realize he's sparked a tingle in your tummy, because those hopeful glances are likely being dismissed by the men looking for a bright as daylight green light from women.

Now on the flip side, women are geared to under- estimate when men are flirting with them. Which means that the man you've been looking for might have been sending smoke signals you unfortunately dismissed as just a   distant brush fire. No wonder you keep passing each other like ships in the night.

I remember going to a house party when I was 16 where a guy I'd had a crush on through high school confessed he'd been crushing on me for the past two years. I could have killed him for saying nothing while I was single, but the fact is I was equally responsible for missing his mooning gaze whenever he looked my way.

So whatever category you might fall under, whether it's shy or confused or homebody, fear not. I have a solution for you.

First, let's address the location issue. Take a good look at your usual haunts: the coffee shop, the bus or subway ride, even around your workplace. If those are too close for comfort and you want to make sure that if things go south you'll never run into him again, that's completely understandable, but you'll have to get out of your comfort zone. If you're not meeting men at your usual gathering spots it's time to widen your roaming territory and get out there. Out where? Anywhere! Just go where the men go.

Try different coffee shops and look for a place that offers an ambiance matching the kind of man you're looking for. Want a casual, no frills man's man? Tim Hortons. Seeking the hipster adventurer? Starbucks. Looking for a studious, slightly intense sort of man? Look for that hole in the wall space where people gather around large, roughly hewn slabs of wood to exchange ideas. Want to shake up your life? Seek out those places where you'd normally never go and find someone there to help broaden your horizons.

Do you love to read? Browse your favourite aisles at local bookstores and watch for wedding ring-free fingers. Want a man who can fix anything around your house? Walk around in a hardware store. Hit the local farmers market and maybe you'll find a foodie like you. Take some classes; you might meet someone who's as adventurous and curious as you are. Get out with friends, and join a bowling league or any other sports team; this will expand your social network. He might not be there, but you might make a new friend who knows someone perfect for you. Watch the local newspaper for trade shows geared towards manly things like sports, home building, outdoor life, or boats and cars. And don't forget that cute man walking down the street might be looking for someone just like you, so don't be afraid to stop him and ask for directions before giving your number or email address.

It's not that there aren't plenty of men out there, and it's not that they're not single and looking for someone great to complement their lives, like you are. Sometimes it's just that they don't know you're available and interested.

CHAPTER 24

Let's Get This Party Started

BEING OPEN TO INITIATING THE DATING DANCE with a man is absolutely vital to your love life. How can you meet a multitude of men from which you'll choose the best partner if your only options are the ones with the courage to approach you first? You're missing out on a ton of other opportunities simply because the rest aren't sure if you're available or receptive. So be obvious.

The best, quickest, and easiest technique I teach is what I call the Hit and Run Flirting method. It's very much like the Victorian style of flirting that women used to start a courtship, sans the handkerchief.

Here's what you do.

You see a man, say, at the coffee shop. Something in your stomach ignites and you feel a flush. This is good, it's your intuition telling you there's something about him that's attractive. It could be his looks or it could be his energy, whatever; right now there's no need to analyze.

If he's close by, turn to him. If he's across the room, go to him. Yes, that's right, go to him. I know, you're nervous and shaking and so afraid you'll mess it up and thinking, *What if I look like a complete idiot?* It doesn't matter. Fear is just a feeling, it's not reality and nothing has happened yet, and you never know. And really, if you do end up tripping over your words (or your feet) you'll have a funny story to tell once you get over your initial mortification. Just do it anyway. This time might be a mess and the next time too, but if you keep at it you'll become more and more comfortable with the process. This will never happen if you don't start, right now.

Next, say the obvious, followed by a question. Is he wearing funky socks? Compliment them and ask where he bought them. Does he smell nice? Say so and ask him what cologne he's wearing. Does he look like he could fix anything around your house? Say so and ask where you'd find more men like him. Does he look like he matches the environment, or seems so opposite from his surroundings he stands out like a moose at a bunny convention? Say so and ask if he comes here often. Don't be afraid of clichés! Just start the conversation; this is your way of dropping that lacy handkerchief and seeing if he's going to pick it up.

Now that you've broken the ice, have a short chat with him. Introduce yourself and ask what he does or if he likes all this snow we're getting, if he's planning on attending a local concert, or if he visits a local park and walks the trails often. Toss him a second question and learn a bit more about him. Ask him if he loves his life and mention any similarities or differences between what he does and what you do. This is a way of creating a small sense of familiarity between the two of you.

Keep it short, just a few minutes, and then it's time for you to go. Why? Because you're a busy woman with things to do and you have to run off now! Even if all you have waiting for you is your dog and Netflix, don't stay and create a first date out of this encounter no matter how great it may turn out. Your goal is to make an impression, establish if this is the sort of man you're interested in, and see if he's interested enough to want to pursue more. If you like him and want to see him again it's up to you to initiate the chase by giving him your contact info, not chase after him yourself.

Wait, what do I mean by initiate the chase?

This is where it's important to understand the psychology of how men operate. So let's journey far back to caveman days again and get in touch with how men are to their core. Back then in order to survive a man had to be strong, confident, and resourceful. Men today still like to exercise those instincts, and if you have any doubt look at any sporting event. Just because we're thousands of years away from our early homo sapien days doesn't mean we've lost all those instincts. Don't you still have the deep set desire to nurture and care for another human being? Then it should be easy for you to understand that real men still have the instinct to hunt for and bring back a prize. It's in their DNA to want to feel accomplished.

Any man will tell you that men will always go after what they really want. It's simply up to you to put yourself on their radar. That being said, after you've had a short conversation with the cutie at the coffee shop it's time to end it and see where things go. If he picks up where you left off you're in the sights of a man who is truly interested in you. If he doesn't then don't chase him. Doing so is like buying a top that's the wrong size just because it's on sale. You got what you paid for: a bargain that doesn't fit right. You want to be with the sort of man who will do whatever it takes to be with you because he finds you special, intriguing, attractive, and a good fit for him. Sounds like a great foundation to me.

So here is your next step: Extract yourself from the conversation by saying, "This was really nice, but I have to run! Can I give you my number (or an e-mail address you created for these encounters), and we'll get together for a coffee sometime?" This is a clear sign that 1) you enjoyed him and 2) you'd like to see him again. If he says no that's fine, you've lost nothing but you've gained experience in flirting. If he says yes, give it to him and if he insists on giving you his number take it, but don't call or text him. You want to be with a man who finds you so interesting he's looking forward to seeing you again and will put in the effort to make plans, not a guy who's waiting around to see who'll make things easy for him.

If you can do this ten times a day, do so. This is your time to open doors and select from who walks through them. The point of this is to start seeing all the possibilities that are out there and to develop that little voice in your head. Don't be afraid of rejection. Remember, it's nothing more than a feeling and when you push that aside there are endless possibilities awaiting you.

Do it over and over and over, because maybe the first man you talk to will call and set up a date, but maybe it'll be the 20th. The fact is, not everyone is a perfect fit and it could take a lot of tries before you meet the man you'll click with. There's work involved in being with a great man, but if you're willing to put in the time and personal growth it's a given you're going to come across him eventually. And like the great hunter he is, he'll work hard to make sure he lands the prize he's got his eye on: you.

What if you've never suffered from shyness and have no problem initiating contact with men? Kudos! I love your courage. Go forth with your newly opened intuition and keep approaching the men you find interesting. Remember, you want to initiate a chase in order to separate the guys from the men. Give them your contact information and see who comes calling for more.

If your cultural norms make approaching men feel taboo, you'll have to overcome that. Until you put yourself in the position of power and choice, you're limiting yourself in the quality of men you can choose from. Give yourself permission to respond to your own personal truth, and if you've been meditating and opening your intuition your heart becomes your best guide. Step outside your comfort zone and soar to new heights. Remind yourself that breaking away from past patterns require you to create new habits and have the courage to speak your truth.

What if you're so tired of being hit on by men that the thought of chatting them up turns you off? Here's the key... you need to start tuning into your intuition and approaching the men that stir up a response. If a man approaches and you don't feel any butterflies, by all means turn him away. If you do though, give him your info and see if he chases. And if you get that flutter when you spot him across the room, don't hesitate. Do the Hit and Run technique. It only takes a few minutes of your time, but it could lead to a lifetime of happy stories with the man of your dreams.

CHAPTER 25
Flirting 101

"WHAT ARE SOME GOOD FLIRTING TECHNIQUES?" is the second most common question I get. Remember in Overcoming Fear when I talked about how body language and tone of voice telegraphs 93% of our communications? There are four uber clear signs men look for when it comes to giving the green light. Here they are:

1) **Eye contact.** We are animals by nature (mammals to be specific), which means we have certain rituals we instinctively pick up on, and eye contact is the biggest one. It's the way we communicate a greeting and clearly signal to each other, "Hello, I'm open to you." Think about how you use eye contact with those you care for and avoid it with the creepy guy in the grocery store aisles. Now think about how you'd use eye contact with the man across the room, the one who's making your heart flutter. Are you too shy to hold his gaze? If so, he has no idea he's having any sort of effect on you. If you want him to realize you're into him and signal your desire for contact, you have to look him in the eye and hold that contact. Otherwise, as far as he's concerned you're just another girl looking around the room. Three seconds is ideal and

make sure you do it at least twice to get the point across. Go ahead and practice in the mirror right now so you can get a sense of what three seconds should feel like. Go to a mirror and turn to the side, then turn your head and look into your eyes for a three second count. Did you smile?

2) **Smile!** You're looking at him. He's looking at you. How does he know you're not just spacing out or looking at him thinking, *Geez, who'd ever wear that?* Your face should communicate what's on your mind, so let it break out in a big, beautiful smile. If he'd love to come over and talk to you this is the sign he's been waiting for. You may feel shy and maybe maintaining eye contact for longer than a second took a huge effort, but he needs to know you really want to talk to him and your smile is what's going to tell him you're ready, willing, and able. Hold his eye and smile, and then do it again. It's the double whammy that eliminates any doubt in his mind. And if he smiles back but doesn't come over, you go over and execute the Hit and Run flirting technique. The ball's in your court. Lob it to whoever you want because at the end of the day talking to as many men as possible gives you the opportunity to choose one who's right for you.

3) **Be coy.** Google Princess Diana and you'll see what I mean. That chin slightly down, steady eye contact, eternal smile: classic flirtatious facial language. It makes men melt, just you watch. A chin up often

signals defiance, so be very conscious of how you're positioning yourself.

4) **Touch.** When it comes to us mammals, touch is how we communicate clear interest in a partner. You can do all the other steps till the cows come home, but his brain is still waiting for the clearest sign of all: your willingness to engage in physical contact. When do you touch him? The moment you know you want to see where things go. If it's during that first conversation, do it then. Reach out and lightly stroke his arm. I call this breaking the bubble because it eliminates the subconscious distance between you. Just one or two touches during your Hit and Run moment is enough, and if you like him when you go on your first date, touch him some more. Touch his arm when you ask a question, when he makes you laugh, when you make him laugh, any time you feel like touching, do it. The more he likes you, the more he'll appreciate the touches he's receiving. Make it the Bat Signal to what's going on in your head.

CHAPTER 26
When Do I Kiss?

THERE ARE A TON OF OPINIONS on when the first kiss should take place, and it's no wonder it's confusing. "You have to kiss on the first date so you know whether there's chemistry." "Wait at least till the third date before you kiss." I don't disagree that the chemistry question can be answered with that first kiss, but maybe, just maybe, the reason you're reading this book is because in the past you let chemistry lead the way before taking some time to figure if this was the right man for you. Maybe now is the time to try something completely different. So if you're ready to try a new trick, here it is.

No kissing for three months.

I know, I can hear you all the way over here. "No kissing? What are you, nuts?" And the answer is nope, just well aware of how our biology works. The fact is, when our lips come together they create a chemical secretion which acts as a strong aphrodisiac called Phenyl Ethylamine (PEA). PEA is super fun, so fun that our bodies treat it the same way it does other amphetamines like Speed, Ecstasy, and Meth. Add a big dose of oxytocin, the hormone your body creates that makes you feel warm and fuzzy, and dopamine, the chemical reaction that acts as your reward signal, and it's no surprise that once kissing happens it's difficult to not get into bed sooner rather than later.

And when you take into account how women traditionally don't kiss more than one man at a time, you can see how that first kiss instantly blocks any other man from having a chance with you—at least until you stop kissing this one. This closes a lot of doors for someone who is still a stranger; it doesn't make sense. Look, would you lend a stranger $1,000? Then why are you handing over your most prized asset, your heart, to someone you don't even know yet?

I know what I'm saying is counter-culture, because kissing within the first few dates is considered the norm. But when you're deciding so soon to close the door on other dating prospects you're putting someone you don't know ahead of someone who could prove to be better for you. And let's be honest, a big part of locking lips early on stems from the fear of losing a potentially good partner to someone willing to offer physical intimacy right away.

But the truth is, this solution is a perfect way to separate the men from the guys. Three months means nothing to the man who's planning on being around for the next 30 years. Three months is too long for the guy who isn't thinking beyond two weeks. The question is, what do you want? A man with long term goals or a guy who's distracted by his immediate urges?

But let's get into the science of what I'm saying. From an evolutionary perspective, how do you think we, as a species, got here in the first place? Because in the natural order of things, we women were the choosers. In fact, with most species on this planet the male has to take the time to show he's stronger, builds a better nest, has brighter colours, and prove that he'll outdo every other male vying for the right to reproduce. If you think asking for time to see if the male in front of you can show his worth will scare off a great potential mate, you're wrong. The one who's got his eye on you because he sees what great qualities you have will take the time to let you realize how great *he* is. If on the other hand he's looking for something quick and easy or doesn't feel he can offer what you're looking for, he'll fade off into the sunset, leaving you free to keep looking for the ideal man.

Why do you want to take on the no kissing for three months rule? Because you're tired of the merry-go-round. Tired of having a great experience the first few dates and locking yourself into a relationship with someone you think could be The One, only to find out a few months later there are major bugs to work out. Tired of spending additional months (or years) trying to sort through the issues that pop up, only to eventually face the fact that you're breaking up because you really weren't compatible in the first place.

Experience has taught me both personally and through my coaching practice that slapping a waiting period on that first kiss avoids a significant number of train wrecks. What's a train wreck? It's what happens when your long term goal of having a loving, committed, happy relationship gets derailed.

When you tell someone you won't kiss for three months you get a very clear idea what sort of potential partner you're dealing with. The guy who says, "Um, I can't wait that long," and stops calling when you stick to your guns is the sort of guy who'll run whenever things get tough. Better to know now instead of later, when you're in love with him, right? And the one who says, "Okay, let me mark my calendar," is showing you not only does he respect you as a person, but he sees long term potential in you. And isn't that what you're looking for, someone who sees themselves with you beyond three months from now because they enjoy what they're discovering about you?

You want to be with someone who wants to be with you, not someone who's just looking to be with someone. You want a man willing to invest the time it takes to understand your wants, your desires, and your favourite foods and flowers because what he's looking for is a woman he can make happy. What you don't want is a guy who likes that it takes minimal effort to be with you because that's all you'll end up getting throughout your relationship – minimal effort. If you set the bar high some men will fail to make the jump, but those who do are the ones who want to prove they're well worth the wait.

Is it hard to not kiss for three months? You bet it is. When you feel that buzz of chemistry with someone and tell yourself you're not going to go for it until you know him much better, it's not like that buzz goes away. With a great man, the more you get into his personality the more you want to kiss him every day, all day long. You keep going in for kisses because it's what you're naturally drawn to do and, if you're like me, you have to keep re-directing your face at the last second. It makes for a lot of moments where you're frustrated and laughing at the same time, because you're waiting for that specific date to finally dive in.

But if you're looking for something different this time around then no kissing for three months will give it to you. What you'll end up with after three months is a man who waited for you to be sure. Sure about who he is, sure about how you feel about him, sure about whether he fits with your lifestyle, your friends, and your family. Sure about whether getting into a relationship with him is a good decision for you. And isn't what reading this book is all about? Learning how to feel certain about the man you choose the next time around?

Setting a specific date also takes pressure off both of you. Say you told him (and yourself), "I'll kiss you when I know you better." Now there's a subconscious pressure on both of you to constantly analyze your feelings and everything that goes on when you're together. He's likely wondering what you're thinking of him and how he can change his behaviours to win you over sooner rather than later, because let's face it, sex is one way he feels he can close this deal with you. Meanwhile, you're constantly riding a roller coaster of emotion because all you're focusing on is how you're feeling moment by moment, wondering if now is the right time to take it to the next level.

By setting a specific date extending beyond the strong biological responses you have when entering a new relationship, and setting a concrete timeframe for getting to know someone better, you give both of your brains an opportunity to relax. The only thing you need to focus on is if you like him, giving you an opportunity to truly get to know each other as human beings. You take the question of *Is it time yet?* completely and clearly off the table, giving yourself a chance to see if you can be friends before raising the relationship to the next level and evolving into lovers. Seriously, doesn't that make sense?

Let me say that again: "Giving yourself a chance to see if you can be friends before raising the relationship to the next level and evolving into lovers."

Happy couples spend their their lives with someone they feel is their best friend.

Don't let fear keep you from setting this boundary or reducing the time-frame (you'd be surprised at how many guys make it to the 2.5 month mark, only to fade off when they realize that you're serious about kissing meaning commitment). Real men, the kind who're willing to commit and deeply love a woman, don't shy from this philosophy and welcome the chance to get to know you before deciding to enter a devoted relationship. They're the ones whipping out their calendar and noting the date for that first kiss (It's true, you'll see). Guys, on the other hand, will try to pressure and cajole their way to early intimacy, hoping this will secure you. You've been down this road before; don't do it again. You lose nothing when you don't fear taking your time, but you risk losing time when you fear losing a stranger.

Men and women who think, *If I don't have sex now I'll lose this person,* are operating from a place of fear and insecurity. If this is how your relationship begins, this is how it will continue. Don't be afraid of losing someone because you're not giving in, and don't let someone else's fear lead you into a relationship with them. Have the courage to use time to your advantage and you'll end up with a man whose security, compatibility, appreciation, love, and ability to connect with you intimately will blow your mind. I have it, I've taught women to find it, and I know you can experience it too. Just don't be afraid.

CHAPTER 27

Making First Dates Comfortable

LADIES, LET ME START THIS SECTION by making sure you're aware of something I call Best Behaviour Syndrome. Best Behaviour Syndrome is how we behave during the first few months of dating, when we feel shiny and new, and our negative qualities like that grumpiness we get when we're hungry (I've lost count of how many times I've had to apologize to my hubby for being hangry) take time to surface. We have a lot of chemicals coursing through our bodies making us happier than usual, and it takes time to re-adjust and get back to normal. We'll even sleep less yet feel more alert. That's the power of your brain on attraction. It's a magical time, but not one to base reality on.

If you allow time for both of you to come back to earth you'll not only see who your dates are for real, but you'll get a chance to discover if they appreciate you for all that you are. And when communicate you want to know him better before initiating even the first kiss you let his brain relax and switch modes, and he can put aside the question of when he's going to have sex and focus on getting to know you.

When should you tell him about your decision to not kiss until you've known him at least three months? On the first or second date. My advice is the moment you think he has potential or the moment he wants to kiss you, whichever comes first, tell him. And telling him isn't as hard as you think.

By the time you'd bring it up there are a few things you already like about him. Does he make you laugh? Is he showing thoughtfulness? Is he a great conversationalist? Does he share your love of watching scary movies on Halloween?

Look him in the eye, and say, "I like you, you're (list what you like and appreciate about who he is), and I want to see where this will go. But I don't get into relationships with people I don't know, and it takes time to get to know someone. I feel three months is long enough, so if we're still seeing each other on (count three months out from either the date of this conversation or the day of your first date) we'll have our first kiss."

Make it clear this decision isn't about him, that's it's simply about your method of making sure you're committing to someone with the potential to be a lifelong partner. Explain that this is your way of gaining clarity, that you know what sort of man you're looking for and you're giving time to let things unfold and see if you two are truly compatible. After your first date send him a text re-stating the qualities you like and appreciate about him. This gives him further reassurance that your decision is more about you and not based on anything he's done wrong, and it reminds him that you really, really do like him, even if you're choosing to not kiss him for a while.

If a guy doesn't stick around for three months or you decide he isn't right for you before the kiss date rolls around, thank your lucky stars you averted a disaster before it happened. And the man you still want to kiss at the three month mark? Let's just say you might have to blockade a distance so no one is injured by the fireworks. What if that first kiss isn't as nice as you'd hoped, because his technique is wayyyyy off? Say to him, "Let me kiss you," then show him what your kissing style is. Men want to please you, and he'll appreciate being with a woman who isn't afraid to show him what she likes.

That being said, what's the best way to engage with him during those first few dates and get to know each other? Start by being as natural as possible. Having first dates over a meal or coffee can be daunting because where else in life are you sitting down with someone who's almost a complete stranger? Maybe during a business meeting, but otherwise it's not something you'd usually do. There's a lot of pressure to perform: to keep the conversation flowing, to find out as much as possible, to be engaging and entertaining nonstop. This in itself can be stressful and tiring, and sometimes things don't go as smoothly as they could have if one of you is a little shy, introverted, or is just having an off day. This first date blunder can halt what could have been a great relationship, simply because we create so much pressure and discomfort early on.

You can ease some of that angst by simply changing the dynamic of your physical bodies. Instead of choosing a date where you'll be facing each other straight on, you can do something where you'll be side by side. Remember the last time you were angry and had a fight with someone? I bet you faced them squarely and let them have it. Now think about a nice, comfortable stroll with someone you enjoy; body positioning plays a big role on your subconscious mind.

Comfortable first dates are those where silences don't become awkward and eye contact isn't forced. By choosing activities where you can allow yourselves to reflect and relax without being expected to constantly say something lets you take in the person you're with. You can save the dinner dates for when you've gained more intimacy and being face-to- face is a pleasurable experience rather than a "Crap, what do we say now?" scramble. It also keeps you from falling into interview mode, which isn't comfortable for anyone.

So go for walking dates. If the weather is co-operating find interesting neighborhoods, parks, zoos, trails, or marinas to explore together. If it's not make dates to go to trade shows, wine tastings, museums, or fun activities like indoor rock climbing. Anything where you're occupied with more than just each other.

If you're enjoying him, touch him. Not kissing doesn't mean you can't have any kind of physical contact. Hold his hand, stroke his arm, put your arms around each other and hug and cuddle as much as you want. Getting to know him means allowing intimacy to grow, and when you communicate, "I'm holding off sexuality until I know you better," you open the door for real intimacy to happen, the kind of intimacy that takes place when you let your humanity to shine through.

Don't have sleepovers during the first three months either. If the chemistry is right and you're enjoying each other it'll be tempting to spend every available minute of the day together. Don't. Maintain your independence, because this space will give you time to reflect and dissect your time

together and catch any red flags that may pop up. It also gives you an opportunity to see if he will respect your independence and willingly give you the ability to be your own person. If he's pushy about spending nights together, beware. This could be someone who will push his agenda over your desire to be happy. Keep yourself open for someone who shows you the utmost respect while looking for ways to make you smile every day.

CHAPTER 28

Dating More Than One Man at a Time

HERE'S ANOTHER REASON why you want to commit to not kissing someone until you've known them at least three months: you don't want to attach yourself to someone who may ultimately be wrong for you and miss out on the one who'd be perfect.

If you're kissing someone chances are you're taking yourself out of the dating scene, and if you're locking yourself into a brand new relationship you're missing out on a ton of possibilities. By not kissing you're still available to go on dates with other men, which means you may have two or three or even more potential partners you can explore simultaneously.

Remember, this is your time to figure out what's right for you, and anyone who insists you lock yourself in before giving a chance to know who they are is displaying controlling and insecure behaviour. If they don't respect you enough to honor what's important to you, in this case wanting to find the ideal partner, this should be your cue to call it quits. A secure man will show you he has enough amazing qualities to win you over, not bully you into committing to him.

You don't need to tell him about anyone else you're seeing, but be honest about the fact that you're not tying yourself down yet if he asks. You want a relationship that's based on truth and communication, so it's okay to be open about your desire to find the right man for you. Don't be afraid of scaring someone off, because the ones you do are the ones who aren't strong enough to be by your side when doing so poses a challenge. Weed them out and be glad you did, because as far as challenges go, getting to know you is the smallest one. If letting you see his true colours before allowing access to your body and soul is too much to ask, then he's not the man for you. If giving you freedom of choice is too much to ask for then he's not the man for you. If allowing time for your relationship to develop is too much to ask, then guess what? He's not the man for you.

I can't stress enough, a man who will be by your side through thick and thin is the one who wants to work hard enough to be the one to win your heart. He won't quit because you're spending time with other men, especially when he knows you're waiting for the right one to kiss. Knowing you value yourself and your goals this much only makes you more valuable in his eyes, because you're showing him you're a strong woman who understands her own worth and the qualities she brings to the table. And strong women don't let strangers rule their world.

Seeing you're the sort of woman who isn't easy to get with and is discerning about where she gives her kisses signals to a man you're looking for a high quality relationship. This gives him comfort knowing that while he may not be the one kissing you today, neither is just any schmo. He'll wait, knowing the best man will win.

CHAPTER 29
What is Physical Attraction?

I LIKE TO BREAK US DOWN into three components when explaining human behaviours: our biological animal, our logical mind, and our spiritual essence.

Your spirituality is something personal for you, and I touch little upon it in this book. What I will say from my own experience, when you let logic and spirit lead the way to a man ahead of biology, you find a love beyond what you could imagine.

Our biological animal drives many of our impulses, and we are designed by DNA to procreate. In a way our bodies are nothing more than vehicles used by DNA to prolong its own existence. Think of Darwin's Theory of Evolution, which explains how DNA will shift the physical make-up of bodies to adapt to changing environments. Look at skin colour for example: Those who live closer to the equator have darker skin protecting them from the sun's rays, while people living in more northern climates have lighter skin to provide efficient production of crucial vitamin D. In the end, all your DNA wants is to survive and make more DNA.

Because of that, your body contains a complex structure called the Endocrine System, a hormone-producing network filled with functions to promote procreation. When we touch each other oxytocin sends us in a wonderful tailspin of delight, making us feel warm and fuzzy, energetic, and forgetful. This is what causes those sleepless nights where all you think about are the great qualities this new partner displays while forgetting the red flags that popped up.

Dopamine is released during physical touch too, and it turns out dopamine is the chemical reaction in our brains which make cocaine such a rush. No wonder when we touch someone all we want is more. The reward center in our brain is sending out huge signals to get as much as we can, as often as we can.

Back when we were cavemen and cavewomen that chemistry (our biological body) took a back seat to our logical minds. Yes, men were attracted to females who could produce a baby strong enough for survival, and women were drawn to males strong enough to protect and provide for the young until they grew enough to run from predators and forage for food. But the deciding factors when choosing a partner weren't just fertility and physical strength, but strength of character too. Devotion and consistency were key because when survival hung on a thread you needed to rely on your mate to stay by your side.

Media has taught us that sex and chemistry belong at the forefront when choosing a relationship, and logic is something we use for fixing problems. But if we go back to our basic natures and use our logical minds before enjoying what our biological bodies offer, those of us who use investigative skills to find the best man end up in happier, more stable relationships. This helps end the cycle of entering relationships and breaking up when they turn out to be incompatible.

By not being afraid of using logic and changing the dynamics of dating you can be more successful at finding love, and once you find a good man the chemistry that was there all along can be unleashed to its full potential with no harm done.

STEP 5

Discover

You've made your list, meditation is ramping up your intuition and confidence, and those flirting techniques are getting you calls for dates. You've been sticking to your No Kissing for Three Months rule and watched as some of the guys you've met disappeared once they realized you're serious about finding a committed relationship. *Good riddance,* you think, because you know if you'd stuck by them they probably wouldn't have stuck by you once things got tough.

Now it's time to really take a good look at who's still around hoping to win your heart. There's a lot to dissect, and though you're clear about who you're looking for you now need to develop a laser-like vision into the men standing before you.

CHAPTER 30

Learning to Let Go

I WENT TO THE KITCHEN to begin dinner while Taylor flipped through his iPod, looking for the perfect music to play. He'd brought a mini-stereo from home, his passion for music leaving him unsatisfied with the outdated Sony cassette and CD player in my living room. Soon I heard music fill my house and I turned to find him standing nearby, idly observing me while a gentle smile played on his lips.

I smiled back at him, filled with appreciation. I loved his thoughtful nature, his giant yet gentle stature, and the way his eyes lit up when he talked about the latest recording artist. He found meaning in the little things, and his qualities made not kissing him so hard to do.

I set my knife down and walked over to him. Wrapping my arms around his waist, I leaned in close and for the hundredth time, went in for a kiss. At the last second I remembered, nope, no kissing yet, and turned my face towards his shoulder. We laughed; it was a common occurrence, and laughing helped ease the tension. We held each other close and just stood there, enjoying the sensations as we allowed ourselves to sink into one another's presence.

I sighed and felt myself relax while he stroked my back, and the music caught us both in its rhythm. We'd met on the sunny dance floor of a boat travelling Toronto Harbour, where my first impression of him was a sense of calm, strength, and safety. I felt it again as we swayed together in my kitchen, and I let our impromptu slow dancing last the duration of the song.

When it finished I sighed again and gave him one more squeeze. I loved that we could share those moments. I appreciated his patience, and his willingness to put kissing on hold so we could learn to share intimacy before becoming sexual showed me how emotionally strong he was too. He was giving me a chance to see what sort of man he was, and so far I was impressed. I added another gold star to his growing collection, kissed him on the cheek before easing out of his arms, and smiled with happiness as I went back to chopping carrots for dinner.

CHAPTER 31

The Nitty Gritty of Narrowing Down Your Options

YOU'RE DATING, and one or two men are standing out and giving you a thrill. I always say, "Life begins when you ask the right questions," and now is the time to ask: Who is this man? Will he be right for me? Is he everything he says he is? Some guys love a challenge, so compare what he says versus what he does. This is another advantage to not kissing for three months: It gives you time and space to weed out the sincere from the manipulators.

What should you watch out for? Let's start with what your 90 Day Checklist should be and tackle each point one by one. Keep these points in mind during your three month "let's see where this goes" period.

#1 – Chemistry: That thing about him that made your knees weak and heart flutter, is it holding steady, increasing in time, or has it fizzled before three months are up? If it goes by the wayside and all you can imagine is watching movies with popcorn instead of tearing his clothes off, then it's time to have the let's just be friends chat. Sometimes chemistry is nothing more than a flash in the pan, and the advantage to waiting is having the opportunity to explore how deep it runs and if it'll last.

#2 – Compatibility: Are you getting along? Do you like enough similar things? Do you have fun when you're together? Are you showing each other new things? Does he consistently make you feel good about yourself and is he expressing how good he feels when he's with you? Does your time together feel harmonious? Does he feel like a good fit? Are you opening up to each other? If you're fighting more often than not, if your time together is punctuated with uncomfortable moments, then say bye-bye; you don't need that kind of negativity in your life. I mean, you haven't even kissed and things are unraveling. Move on, and find someone you can expand on the enjoyment of life with. Be true to yourself; this is not the time to compromise on essentials.

#3 – Shared Values: Are your values matching up? Do you both want kids (or not)? Are you both on board with the notion that farts are funny? Is he as dedicated to family as you are or, if not, does he support your desires to spend time with your family? Is he open-minded? Does he enjoy and dream about enough of the same things you do, giving you hope that one day you can do them together? Does he share the same faith you do, or at least support your beliefs even if they're not his? In essence, does he value what you value? If not he might be best reassigned to the friend-zone, because the things you hold dear that he doesn't care about will cause fights, or as I like to call them, heated negotiations. Starting a relationship on the right foot means ensuring you have a solid foundation to work from, and if your values don't match up you're chipping away at the pillars that support the whole structure.

#4 – Compatibility with Your Core People: Does he get along with the people you love and do they like him? Those who know you best and love you most have your best interest at heart. Sometimes we get caught up in the initial magic and turn a blind eye to red flags that pop up, so listen to what your inner circle has to say about him and pay attention to what he says about them. If he has trouble getting along with them and is trying to make you choose "them or me," don't stand for it and let him go.

Guys with a tendency to be abusers will want to separate you from loved ones to gain a greater measure of control over you. The only exception to this rule is if you've surrounded yourself with an unhealthy entourage of users and abusers, and if that's the case it's time to fix that before getting into a relationship. You need to repair your leaky roof before renovating your kitchen because otherwise you're wasting your time and resources.

A lot of people have rules about when they want to introduce children to those they date. My advice is, find out early if you get along with his kids and if he gets along with yours. Because you're not kissing but instead just hanging out and getting to know each other there's a significant amount of relationship drama that isn't introduced during this timeframe. Use this time to really see if you'd fit well into each other's lives.

#5 – Respect: Is he respecting your time? Your space? The words coming out of your mouth? Is he listening when you set boundaries? If you tell him not to call or text after 11p.m. because you need your beauty sleep and he's texting "I miss you" at 11:30, he's not listening to you. Be aware when he's overstepping the needs you lay out for him. It might seem romantic at first but the best predictor of   future behaviour is past behavior. If he's showing you what you say doesn't matter because his wants supersede your needs you'll end up fighting over bigger issues down the road.

If you tell him, "I don't kiss for three months," and he keeps trying to force a kiss, he's not respecting your boundaries. If he sets up dates, then cancels and makes last minute plans to make up for it he's not respecting your time. If you tell him certain behaviours like burping bother you and he keeps doing them, he's not respecting your comfort zones. Little things become big things, so keep an eye out and don't be afraid to let him know you don't stick around for that kind of behaviour when they start to add up.

#6 – Consistency: We're all guilty of being over- idealistic at some point in our lives but if he's drawing big pie in the sky scenarios and not backing them with actions then run, don't walk, out the door. "The road to hell is paved with good intentions," said St. Bernard De Clairveaux, and surely he had a few of my ex-boyfriends in mind when he wrote that. While you may be swept up in his larger-than-life personality or sweet sounding dreams, giving yourself time to see if they materialize is the wisest thing you can do. Some guys want to woo you with romantic ideals of where you can end up together, but when you force them to put their money where their mouth is they realize it'll take more than words to win your heart. Wait to see if their dreams become reality before believing anything you hear. If it sounds too good to be true, it more than likely is.

Keep an eye out for consistency of behaviour too. He might have been uber polite to you and wait staff for the first two months, but if it morphs into rude behaviour break it off. If at first he always insisted in picking you up for dates but now wants you to chauffeur, this is a sign he's not who   he started out as. If you yearn after two-and-a-half months for the person you first met then let it go and look elsewhere for a partner. He's showing you who he is and you can't change him. Accept what is and find a man who'll be solid and steady instead of someone who can change so much in a short period of time.

#7 – Lifestyle Compatibility. Look at all the things that make up your day-to-day life. Do you like going for walks, watching the same sort of TV shows or movies, or enjoy a certain amount of socializing? Do you like travelling and exploring new destinations every year, or love the comfort of old haunts? What are the important things you'd like to share with a partner? Being with someone who doesn't enjoy the sort of activities you do means you'll be flying solo more often than not, and this can cause loneliness in a relationship. Be honest with yourself about whether you'll be okay doing those things alone or find someone who'll be with you if you need to. If you dream of having a partner by your side while enjoying your favourite activities, don't give that up.

Keep referring to this checklist as you tick down the days to your first kiss and make sure you're keeping a clear head and 20/20 vision before committing to anyone. Be open and honest about who you are and what you want from a relationship; the man who falls in love with your truth is the one creating a foundation for the lasting, loving, and committed relationship you want.

CHAPTER 32

Reel Him in Without Scaring Him Off

DATING CAN BE BOTH SCARY AND EXCITING. It's hard to not become jaded when you meet and dismiss one guy after another, and it's equally hard to not turn into an over-enthusiastic freakazoid when you finally meet a man showing potential. If he's fulfilling most of your Perfect Man List it's like hitting a million dollar jackpot in Vegas, but here's the thing: He might still be waiting to see if you're going to be The One for him too, and if you go overboard your enthusiasm could scare him off.

Men are practical in nature and their brains work at a different level than ours. They have an easier time separating their hormonal desires from their emotions, and they're geared to be highly selective when committing to a mate versus simply sleeping with them. Men are typically more comfortable when they're single, because their inner caveman knows once they choose someone to settle down with it's going to require more of them in terms of procuring resources and providing protection.

Women, on the other hand, are less comfortable being single because their inner cavewoman knows there's strength in numbers, and being attached to a caveman means increased safety and resources.

So how do you balance both your lizard brains when pursuing someone?

First, control your impulses. You might want to reach out and talk to him a lot, but if you overwhelm him with attention it means he doesn't get a chance to come forward and meet you where you are. You want to be with a man who's had the opportunity to chase you, because at the end of the day he's going to gain satisfaction answering yes to the question, *Did I earn what I have?* If he gets so much attention it outweighs the effort he's put in, this will be a turn off for him.

Pay close attention to how much he communicates and what he does, and while it's okay to go slightly above and beyond his efforts it's not okay to go massively overboard compared to his actions. If he took you through the McDonalds drive-through for dinner and the next night you're treating him to the best restaurant in the city, he's going to wonder why you devalue yourself because when he does the math his $8 McMeal earned him an $80 steak dinner. If he texts "I had a good time" after your second date and you reply with a novel about how you've never felt so happy and fulfilled, he's going to wonder why it takes so little to sweep you off your feet.

Keep yourself in check and do your gushing with your girls. Unburden your emotional roller coaster with people who will listen in a supportive way, but keep a level of reservation with this new man. He's not going to understand if you start talking about seeing forever in his eyes before you know who he is, and he'll interpret your actions as low self-esteem.

On the flip side, if you're dating someone who's saying he sees forever in your eyes before three months is up be wise enough to dismiss it for the time being. You're still strangers to each other, and it's possible he's laying a bed of verbal rose petals at your feet, hoping you'll follow the trail to his bed. Don't fall for it. Let him know, "That's nice to hear," but keep your eye on the first kiss date and stick to your guns. No kissing for three months keeps you from falling head-over-heels for someone saying all the right things to hide the fact he's actually all the wrong ones.

Learn to recognize and respond to his emotional tides. *Men Are From Mars and Women are From Venus* by John Gray taught me how to recognize and be comfortable with a man's tendency to be plugged in one day and withdrawn the next. John compares this to a rubber band: Even though it can stretch out it will always want to snap back. I see this in my husband: He goes through phases of being super lovey dovey and connected, followed by a stage where he'll be quiet, reserved, and withdrawn.

This is okay. Repeat after me, "Space in a relationship is okay." Men have cycles too, and by giving space and patience during those times we allow them to seek us out when they're ready. I don't push my husband for communication or affection when he retreats. I allow him to mentally go to his man cave for rejuvenation. Once he comes out he's ready to fill himself with love and affection again, and I get to benefit from his strengthened desire to be plugged into our relationship.

When you give someone space during any stage of a relationship, whether it's the courting period or ten years in, you're giving compassion by allowing them to explore themselves without fear of reprisal. This fosters a sense of gratitude and connection. Gratitude because they don't have to be constantly rising up to your expectations, and connection because when you allow someone to be and evolve at their own pace they feel understood and loved, and who doesn't appreciate being with someone who gets them?

And whatever you do, don't tell him what the perfect husband material looks like unless he asks. This is your getting to know each other period, not the time to lay out everything you'll expect him to be. You want him to develop a longing to step up and be the perfect man for you, and you'll recognize this shift when he asks questions like, "So what are you looking for in a man?"

If you start talking about everything you expect from a partner before he's mentally prepared to fill those shoes you're going to overwhelm him. If he's still trying to figure out who you are and you're talking about how he's going to have to be everything your exes weren't, he might feel you're too high maintenance because he's comparing what you need with what he's willing to offer right now. Give him time to create a want inside of him. A want to be the man for you, a want to fulfill your dreams, a want to step up and be everything you're looking for.

CHAPTER 33
Text Him Like a Pro

"SHOULD I WRITE HIM BACK RIGHT AWAY?"
"What should I say when I text him?" "Should I text him first?"

Oh, the torture of those first few months! You're walking a tightrope, trying to balance what you want to do versus society's confusing messages. "Be bold! This isn't the dark ages." says one side. "Be demure! Make men chase." says the other. What's right and what's wrong?

You want to show a man you're interested, but you don't want to come across as desperate. Here are texting tips that will help you strike a balance.

1 – Once he's made contact after your initial meeting and taken you on a date, send him a text saying something sweet or invite him out, and give him the opportunity to respond. You're too valuable to be spending your time trying to corral a guy into being with you. If he takes longer to reply than you'd like, tamper down those antsy fingers and worries he didn't get the message and continue to wait. If he didn't get your text and he's into you, he'll reach out and make sure he's maintaining contact. If he received your last message and isn't

sure if he wants to respond, sending him another one is just chasing after him.

2 – Hold back those epic lines of poetry about his beautiful soul a little while longer and let him lead the way regarding how much to share via text. If you send him messages that are lovey-dovey-smoochey-poochey in response to perfunctory messages about where to meet and how to get there he'll feel you're too emotionally invested, which could either scare him off or give the impression you're desperate. Take a deep breath and let the moment pass.

3 – Make your texts worth waiting for. There's a cute quote I found on the internet saying, "I want to be the reason you look at your phone and smile." Make sure when you text him something it'll trigger his happy place. If you know he does everything he can to spend time with you send a text inviting him to join you somewhere. Write him a short note letting him know you're thinking about him, or send a picture of something that reminded you of what you talked about. Craft a short and sweet thank you text after a fabulous date, telling him you had a great time and are looking forward to seeing him again.

4 – Don't demand to be entertained, and don't be his time filler. Men process and use one fourth of the words we do, so it's no surprise too many questions can feel overwhelming. Save your questions for when you see him face-to-face, because what you want is a man making the effort to spend enough face time to get to know you. Don't get caught up in

answering a million questions over text either. If he's not willing to make space in his life for your physical presence he's not putting in enough elbow grease to earn you.

5 – Don't accept last minute invitations. At least not for the first few months. Remember, you're a fabulous woman living a fabulous life, it's not like you're sitting around waiting for someone to improve your existence. What you're looking for is someone who'll be a great fit. So if he sends a text asking if he can come over (booty call alert!) or if you can get together tonight or tomorrow, gracefully decline while letting him know you'd still love to see him—when he plans ahead. Something like, "I'd love to, but I have something going on already. But I'm free (whatever day is at least three days out) if you want to do something?"

Do you say no even if you have nothing going on? Damn tooting you do. Remember, you need to behave your way to success, and when you allow yourself to be a time filler rather than someone he pursues and craves you become a short term option to his lizard brain.

If he plans dates further out it means he's interested in you. If he doesn't, consider this a red flag. He may be lazy and have little interest in thinking beyond the next day, which is not someone you want to be trying to plan a life with. He may have other attachments and be using you to fill time slots that don't get picked up by other girls. Or he may be slightly interested, but not interested enough to pursue you... yet.

Whatever the case, make planning ahead part of your requirements.

This tactic keeps you from wasting time being someone's short term option and lets guys know you're looking for the man who sees you in his future life, not just his present day.

6 – Be clear. If he texts "let's get together this week, when are you available?" don't reply "maybe Friday" when what you really mean is "I'd love to get together Friday." Men are literal creatures, and some may be shy and unwilling to push. When you reply in a vague way it doesn't necessarily increase their drive to hunt you. He may interpret your words to mean you're not interested, and the man who's into you might turn away because he doesn't want to bother you. If you like him, let him know. If you want to see him, be clear about that. You want a relationship filled with clear communication, kindness, and compassion, right? So lay that foundation from the beginning and see if he can build on it.

7 – Be patient. When it comes to building a house if you rush the foundation you're building on a shaky platform. It's okay to allow time and space between communication and dates. He may be checking out other options, like you should be. These early months are about seeing if the person you're getting to know will be the right one to commit to, not about committing. Don't create an expectation he should reply within a certain timeframe or make another date within a day of your last one. Be fluid, allow things to flow and progress slowly. Let him realize that compared to whatever else is out

there, you're the most mature, most patient, most understanding, most interesting woman he'll find. Let him run his course and come to you naturally. Just like you don't want a man to bully you into a relationship with him, you shouldn't be bullying him into committing to you. Set your expectations aside and simply observe.

If he floats away that's okay. Remember, you're looking for the man who'll fall in love with you and all your qualities. Maybe he understands you're fundamentally different people. Maybe he feels you're looking for a man who'll invest more than he's willing to give. Whatever the case, in the long run you're better off without him, so don't mourn the loss of something you never had. This is why it's vital to not attach too much importance to any one person in the early stages and to be open to dating more than one man at once. The dating dance is a ritual of finding a partner who's swaying to the same rhythm as you, something that only time can tell.

CHAPTER 34
Whatever You Do, Don't Fall Victim to the Pitbull Syndrome

AHHHH, THE PITBULL SYNDROME. We've all been there at some point. It's what happens when you stay because you're waiting for the payoff, holding on and refusing to let go because you think having something between your teeth today surely means you'll gain something to digest tomorrow.

We humans have a subconscious tendency to feel we'd rather stay the course no matter what, gambling with the possibility of losing more long term in lieu of walking away from our initial investment, regardless of how badly things are going. If you've ever bought a movie ticket and sat through two hours of tedium because, damn it, you spent twenty bucks, that's Pitbull mentality. What you're not realizing is you just sold two hours of what could've been more enjoyable time for twenty dollars.

Researchers call this an escalation of commitment, where you'll convince yourself to stay the course despite ever increasing negative outcomes. I know I've been guilty of this in the past, hoping those first three months of honeymoon period re-materialize despite the growing number of fights.

But here's the thing: Giving up now doesn't mean you're giving up on having a great relationship. It means you're acknowledging this particular one, given it's not working out, will likely not turn out the way you'd like. And that's okay. There're a lot of men to discover; it's just a matter of exploring until you find the right one.

CHAPTER 35
Find Out the Truth

STEVE HARVEY WROTE A BRILLIANT BOOK on decoding men, *Act Like a Lady, Think Like a Man.* He tells us to ask men our most burning questions three times, on three different occasions, in three different ways.

Why?

Because their first answer will be what they hope will impress you the most. Remember, you're deep in the Best Behaviour Syndrome phase of your relationship, so what seems like reality actually isn't yet. Being aware of this and taking everything with a grain of salt is wise during those first few months because you're both speaking your ideals more than your deep down darkest truths.

So the first time you get answers to your questions, hear them, but keep an open mind.

Because the second time won't necessarily be the full truth either.

Why?

It's possible the second answer might still be what he thinks will excite you. Remember, he's still trying to impress you.

When you ask him a third time, usually what's left is the truth. This may be the answer you least want to hear, but the one you most have to believe. Don't put blinders on and dismiss this last one because it doesn't live up to what you want. Filtering can be your worst enemy during the discovery period, so don't dismiss answers that fail to live up to your expectations or desires, and face the truth.

CHAPTER 36
15 Discovery Period Questions That Will REALLY Peel His Onion

IT'S HARD TO GET TO KNOW SOMEONE if you don't know how to peel back their layers, and these are great questions both of you can answer during this discovery period. They get beyond the surface and help you uncover who he is while giving him a view into who you are too. When you honestly reveal yourself you give someone the ability to accept you for who you are.

Don't be afraid to write these questions on cards and take them with you on dates. You can use them as conversation pieces when you're having dinner.

#1 – "What do you hate most about the dating process?" He might say, "Having to put pants on to leave the house," and you can bond over your love of track pants and chilling. Or he may say, "The uncertainty of where things will go," showing you a vulnerable side. Awwww.

#2 – "Have you figured out your calling in life? What is it?" This is a look deep into his soul and seeing what resides there. Is he passionate about something or feeling lost?

Share what your dreams and goals are. Compare what he says to what he's actually doing.

#3 – "What were you like as a kid?" Usually we're more developed versions of our younger selves, but those first few dates are so scary that our true natures are sometimes buried. This gives you a peek into his nature, and you might get an answer that shows you he's willing to grow. Maybe you'll hear a story about transformation from shy kid to CEO.

#4 – "Do you have any pet peeves?" If you really like to let your bodily functions do their thing and he hates any indication you digest you're going to be spending your life suppressing yourself. Or if he hates pet hair and you have two fur babies, this might be a sign things are going to get rough. Don't gloss over major incompatibilities just because you want to be with someone. Use this question to see if there are things you'd have to compromise on.

#5 – "Who was your favourite teacher? Why?" Everyone has one or two teachers who stood out at some point, and what we loved is usually something we can relate to. Mine was Mr. Barrie, a big, gentle man who always wore a purple crochet beret and vest, and lo-and-behold I tend to be someone who does her own thing no matter what the world thinks is normal. This is a good way to see who they are deep inside.

#6 – "What should I know about you that I'm not thinking to ask?" Let's all do this together now, "Ooooooo."

This is a good one! It's a great way of unlocking a tidbit he's been hoping to share about himself but hasn't found the opportunity yet.

#7 – "What was your family like growing up?" Pay attention to what he says. If he comes from a loving, secure, bonded family, you can expect he'd want the same environment. Or he may come from dysfunction, which means he'll need to work harder to have harmony. This doesn't mean it's impossible. Just know he'll have baggage that he'll need help unpacking if he hasn't done most of the work already.

#8 – "Did you – or do you – have a nickname? What's the story behind it?" This can be a way of uncovering something fun about him.

#9 – "What's your favourite way to spend a Saturday?" Dating is not how life is naturally lived, and this question helps you discover how he likes to spend his weekends. Are you downtime compatible?

#10 – "What's your biggest goal in life right now?" Does he have goals? Now is a great time to find out. See if your goals are compatible, like buying a house someday or travelling somewhere new every year. Or maybe his goal is to just have a peaceful, calm, serene life, and that sounds like a slice of heaven for you. Find out if what he wants to achieve for himself matches your personality.

#11 – "What's your favourite place in the world?" This clues you into what he finds beautiful and engaging with the world, and it helps you see how deep he can be.

#12 – "What's your favourite movie/book? Why?" Does he like thrillers, comedies, horror stories, or is he a deep thinker that prefers to deconstruct more complicated themes? This question gives insight into the workings of his mind.

#13 – "Who is your best friend? What do you like about him/her?" This might be the moment where you find out the man you're seeing has a frat boy personality, or he creates lifelong bonds. Remember, our friends are a reflection of who we are, so pay attention to this answer.

#14 – "Who is the biggest influence in your life" We seek to follow in the footsteps of those we most respect, so who does this man look up to?

#15 – "What kind of things make you laugh?" A fun question to find out if he has a dark or light sense of humour, and if he cracks up at the same things you do.

CHAPTER 37

Is He a Guy or a Man?
12 Ways To Know The Difference

"OH MY GOD, I'm so tired of dating guys who (fill in the blank)" If you're reading this book you've probably said this at least once in your life. How can you tell the difference between a guy and a man? Watch his behaviour. Here are 12 things to look out for:

#1 – Validation: Guys tend to have multiple women they flirt with (or date), because each one strokes a part of his ego. His insecurities are so deep-set that just one woman's admiration isn't enough to keep him feeling satisfied.

Men are too busy achieving goals or delving into soul-satisfying hobbies to have several women on the go. They'd rather choose one woman to keep happy while rounding themselves in other ways. The most important thing is knowing their efforts are appreciated by the woman they love.

#2 – Jealousy: Guys are very territorial because they fear losing your attention to another male. They'll be suspicious of male friends and will want to convince you that you shouldn't have any.

Men are secure and trust you enough to let you decide for yourself who is and isn't right for you as a friend. My husband likes to say, "I don't want to be with anyone who doesn't want to be with me." By giving me freedom and choice he's assured I'm with him because I want to be, not because he bullies me.

#3 – Appearances: Guys love insecurity because they make you easy to control, but they themselves lack self-confidence. If they have to have the flashiest phone, watch, car, TV, etc. it's usually in the name of playing the one-up game. Their feelings of inferiority play on their minds, and they consciously or subconsciously insist on being perceived as better through the things they have, rather than taking time to earn respect and admiration with their personality.

Men choose to be valued for their character. They surround themselves with people who understand and appreciate who they are and don't care to impress people with stuff. Not to say that men won't have nice stuff, but what they have is not the standard by which they want to be measured.

#4 – Selfishness: Guys will have a what's in it for me attitude and focus on what serves them without regard for other people. They'll fail to see what others do for them, often complaining about how their efforts aren't rewarded enough.

Men are generous with those they care for and will put themselves after family and close friends.

#5 – Control: Guys are easily recognized by their controlling behaviours. They don't take into account what's important to you and make you feel guilty if you don't spend your time and money on them. Need to pay your bills? Well, you obviously don't care about him if you don't pay his debts first. You want to see your sister, who hasn't been doing well lately? Certainly you're not interested in being with him if you're not making him a priority. Do you see what I mean?

Men want you to lead a rich and fulfilling life, however that may be. They have a fundamental understanding that when you're happy you'll bring that happiness home and plant the seed in his garden, growing something you'll both be able to enjoy. Their most common question is, "What do you want?"

#6 – Responsibilities: Guys will complain or even scheme to ditch their responsibilities towards work, children, friends, and exes they're obliged to support. Because they're so focused on their own gratification anything that gets in the way is a source of annoyance to them.

Men will man up and look after their responsibilities with pride and effort. They'll work long hours to achieve more than the average man and spend as much time as possible with their kids, seeking to have a positive influence before they become independent. They'll be generous with the mothers of their children and step in to ensure their kids have secure and reliable housing, activities and medical aid covered, and necessities paid for, knowing doing so contributes to their child's sense of stability and happiness.

#7 – Affection: One indicator of dating a guy is how hard it is to win his affections. In a relationship with a man love and appreciation come freely but   guys make you feel like you must earn scraps of their love. If you have to keep buying things, paying for dinners, or be so easy to be around that you can't even voice an opinion, run. Staying in this relationship will be so draining you'll end up feeling empty.

#8 – Effort: Guys like to gain maximum benefits with minimal effort. Does he own a house? Does he have a steady job he works hard at? Or does he work just enough to cover his basics, leaving it to others to pick up the tab?

Men will show effort in many areas of their lives, believing that hard work gets them ahead. They love achieving as much as they can and take satisfaction from earning what they have.

#9 – Finances: Guys are notoriously bad with money, living in a here today, gone tomorrow kind of world. They manipulate their surroundings in such a way that there's someone else to pick up the bill and don't feel it necessary to save for a rainy day. When a guy comes into a pile of money it's quickly gone, spent on frivolous things like fancy cars or gadgets. He might even spend some on you, but he'll be asking you to foot the bill as soon as the cash runs out, which won't take long.

Men keep a keen eye on long term goals and have no problem saving enough to make sure their expenses are covered. It takes a disaster to put a man into financial trouble because the last thing he wants is to be a burden on someone else.

#10 – Blame: Guys don't like to take responsibility for the negativity in their lives. It's someone else's fault the rent didn't get paid. It's someone else's fault their car broke down. It's certainly your fault you two are fighting. No matter what the circumstance, it can always be twisted in such a way that blame falls on anyone's shoulders but theirs.

Men, well, men have egos too, so while they don't lay blame on others for the more technical issues it may take time to see where they contributed to relationship obstacles. What they will do is agree to work through tough times with you, consenting to counseling to fix problems.

#11 – Paying: Guys might be generous at first, but that soon drops off, and you'll be reaching for your wallet while he pretends to ignore the bill.

Men on the other hand are ready to fight you to the death for the tab. Their instinct to protect and provide means they'll be mortified if you pay for them more than they treat you, and if their finances are low they'd rather stay home than have you take them out.

#12 – Happiness: Guys are all about their own happiness and rarely ask what makes you happy.

Men want you to be happy and when you're not, they're not. It's in a man's DNA to look for happiness in a woman's face because when a mother thrives so does her children, and the cycle of a man providing for a woman's happiness keeps our species flourishing.

Now that I've laid out twelve ways you can tell if you're looking at a guy or a man, keep one thing in mind – nobody's perfect. It's unreasonable to expect any one person to be all twelve of those things and be The Perfect Man, although if you find that unicorn you'd better do everything you can to keep him. But if he's mostly guy move on and find someone else, or set higher standards and see if he turns himself into a man by rising to meet them.

What about you? Take a look at this list again and substitute guy with girl, and man with woman. If you're a girl, then men won't be looking to make long term plans with you. Remember, like attracts like, and men are looking for women who'll be able to complement their long term goals. Do some personal work and attract the man you want; the last thing you want to be is a guy magnet.

That being said, never, ever compromise your physical safety. The moment a guy puts his hands on you, it should be over. No ifs, ands, or buts. The best predictor of future behaviour is past behaviour, and if he feels entitled to do it once he'll feel entitled to do it again, and that's not okay nor something you should ever allow. Not for one second.

There are way too many other men out there for you to be wasting your preciousness on someone who would so blatantly disrespect you. Don't allow for tears or apologies or excuses. End it and move on. If you have trouble doing that, then get help. We are all sisters, and when you allow this sort of pain to your soul we all feel it in our own.

Help yourself, and take care of your beautiful spirit by never letting anyone drag it down to the ground so they can step on it. Love yourself as much as we all love you. Reach out to your local resources and vow to never allow a person to disrespect your body and soul. Help is always available to give you the support and tools to lift yourself up. Take them and fly.

CHAPTER 38

Will a Man Wait for a Woman Who Isn't Giving It Up?

THE SHORT ANSWER IS, YES. Guys won't and that's good, because guys aren't worth your efforts anyway. How many times have you spent years in a relationship only to end up thinking, *Wow, what a waste of time that was!* When you look at my twelve ways to gauge if he's a guy or a man, was he a guy after all?

The biggest difference between guys and men is patience. Guys live to gratify the moment while men diligently work towards their goals.

Ever hear of the Stanford marshmallow experiment led by Walter Mischel? Researchers put four-year-olds alone in a room with a marshmallow, telling them, "You can eat it if you like, it's your marshmallow. But I'm coming back in twenty minutes, and if you haven't eaten it I'll give you a second marshmallow." What this experiment revealed was what level of impulse control the child had, and what you want is the man who can wait for two marshmallows.

Because men are more steady and stable than guys, waiting for sex doesn't put them off. In fact, when you tell them you're not going to jump into bed with someone you barely know they understand you value yourself too much to get involved with someone who doesn't meet your standards. Men understand standards, because they demand such high ones of themselves every day.

By telling them they'll have to take time to put the proof in the pudding you give them a choice. If they're ready for a long-term commitment and they see possibility in you, they'll take the time to stay and prove their worth. Some men aren't ready for something long term though, and this gives them the opportunity to be honest about that.

Listen carefully to what they say, and believe them when the words "I'm not ready to settle down right now" come out of their mouths. Don't give up sex hoping to change their mind. This does *not* work and only devalues you in his eyes. If he's not ready for a commitment right now say your goodbyes, and if you've sparked an interest in him he'll come calling back when he's ready. Then you can start your three month no kissing rule, getting to know him and seeing if he's right for you.

Guys, and men, will take up the offer of free sex when it's presented to them. Of course they would! For them sex doesn't mean a commitment unless you require it of them in order to get the sex. And here's the thing, ladies: They may wonder if you're having sex because you want some fun-fun, but they won't ask in case you're actually fishing for a long term relationship and using sex as the lure. Why won't they ask? Because if the answer is yes and they're not ready for that, they risk losing out on sex because they'll have to be honest and tell you a relationship is not on their agenda. So they play the "shhhhhhh... just let it happen" game until either you or he gets tired.

If you're looking for your forever home with a man you need to weed out the ones who are just looking for sex. Again, this is where waiting three months for a kiss is your best friend, because it's the action that backs up the words "I'm looking for the man who'll be my lifelong partner, and nothing else. If that's your goal too then stay and play, but if not I'm not wasting my time and efforts on you." When it comes to getting into the relationship you want boundaries and honesty are the key to the door. Be honest with yourself and with the person in front of you and you'll get what you want much faster than if you were playing hoping games with someone.

Clearly define your goals and objectives, and be gracious about his.

Once they're ready for a long-term commitment men will be looking for the woman who will stay and grow with them, and they're looking for as many special qualities in a partner as you are. Don't be afraid to make them wait because in reality they're going to appreciate the time to figure you out too. Understand that being clear and scaring away the guys means you'll be available for that special man when you meet him.

CHAPTER 39
Watch Out! Red Flag Alert!

TAKING THREE MONTHS BEFORE KISSING is your time to observe whether you're dating a guy or a man. This is not a probation period to see if he'll accept you; this is when you see if committing to this person is a good idea for you or if you should focus your attention somewhere else.

It's hard enough to see reality for what it is when we're all a-flush with oxytocin and dopamine, (Is there a reason why the word "dope" is in that neurotransmitter's name? Let's file that under "things that make you go hmmmm"). So keep in mind what's happening when you meet someone you like and start engaging in physical contact. By limiting the amount to anything under kissing you're still releasing a lot of yummy oxytocin, but not so much that you'll be blind to red flags.

So what red flags should you be looking for?

First, are you meeting his friends and family? Sure, it may take a while before he brings you out and into his fold, but if it hasn't happened in three months' time it means you're a secret. Huge red flag. Why would you be a secret?

It could well be that yours is not the committed relationship he's looking for, or that he may already be in one.

A lot of women ask me, "Chantal, how can I know if he's married?" You can't know just because he says he's single, and a lot of women complain they date someone only to find out later he's married. But by setting and standing by a three month rule you can see whether he integrates you into his world. If it doesn't happen in three months, adios amigo.

Second, does he take you to his place? If not, what's he hiding? It could be a wife and kids. If you don't go to his place within three months you're not in a relationship. At least not in his mind. Perhaps his excuse is "it's too messy." Even if that were the truth you don't want to spend the rest of your life picking up after a man-child who can't clean up enough to invite the lady he's interested in over for drinks. Move on. A real man makes an effort to create a nice nest for a woman he's wooing.

Third, is he consistent in his behaviours? If he ends up a different person from the one you initially met, chances are you're in for a load of unpredictability going forward. Was he saying sweet nothings in the beginning but now makes passive aggressive comments about how your jeans fit? Leave this one in your rear-view mirror because character and stability are what you're looking for, not a Jekyll and Hyde type of guy.

You could meet someone who hits all 12 of the man points from my "Is He a Man or a Guy?" examples, but if he's showing any of these three traits, watch out. Your red flag alarm should be beeping like crazy; don't ignore them now and regret it later.

CHAPTER 40

Don't Ever Take Yourself Off the Pedestal

TOO MANY WOMEN express discomfort with the notion that a man would put them on a pedestal, not realizing this is where they need to reside to be in the relationship they're looking for. Allowing a man to put you on a pedestal simply means being appreciated and cherished as the amazing woman he sees when he looks at you. But overwhelmingly, women nowadays suffer from cognitive dissonance, where your mind is being pulled in two different directions at once. You want to be cared for in such a way that makes you feel loved and appreciated, but part of you is uncomfortable with the way real men show they care about you.

Here's how I explain this phenomenon: Think of a smoker. She looooooves that cigarette, how it feels between her fingers, the sensation of the smoke going down her airways, watching the smoke come out as she exhales, and the gratification each time she lights up and takes that first puff. But she hates how it's making the skin on her face and neck sag, the dirty looks her kids give her because they know better and think she should too, and the fear one day her game of Russian roulette will end with a horrible disease. Those opposing thoughts in her mind when she lights up is cognitive dissonance.

To be open to the love you're looking for you need to deal with your cognitive dissonance, the part of you that wishes for yet rejects being treated like a Queen. Notice I didn't say "get over it?" That's because I understand whatever is making you uncomfortable when you're being showered with complements and special treatment is probably so ingrained, you're likely dealing with an uphill battle when it comes to overcoming it. But you can; it's just a matter of baby-steps.

Start by analyzing your own behaviour and requiring yourself to stop rejecting acts of kindness. I was watching TV the other day when a woman was given a new car, and the first words out of her mouth when the surprise was revealed were "God no!" Witnessing this made me sad for her, because it was obvious her deepest truth was *I don't deserve the goodness that comes my way.* Train yourself to open up to the positive elements life offers by making Yes! your new inner mantra. Every time someone pays you a compliment or offers you a gift, whether it's flowers or a big night on the town, repeat Yes! in your mind until you bypass your feeling of embarrassment or unworthiness and can simply be grateful. The Universe knows you are deserving; honor it and accept the love it's trying to shift your way.

Next, alter how you view yourself in these situations. You may think allowing a man to treat you weakens your independence and makes you seem incapable of bearing the financial burden of dating. This is not what the man trying to woo you is thinking. And in no way does it demean everything you've been building for yourself. Men pay   for dates to let a woman know he values her time, companionship, and the opportunity to show her what a great man he is, that's all. He isn't seeking to pull your achievement rug out from under you, and you exhibiting defensiveness around these situations confuses him. Relax your mind and allow yourself to flow with him; the right man will appreciate the freedom to express himself.

Remember what Captain Jack Sparrow says in the Pirates of the Caribbean: "The problem is not the problem, the problem is your attitude about the problem." Reduce the importance you ascribe to who pays for what when dating, and you'll open a whole new set of doors in your love life.

I often hear women at my seminars saying, "I can take care of myself; I'm uncomfortable letting someone else pay." What they're talking about is that squishy feeling in the pit of their stomach when they're on a date with a man who insists on treating her to the night out. I know you want to be with a good man, but if you're uncomfortable with the level of care that means accepting you're dealing with cognitive dissonance. Understand that if you want to be with a man who'll be focused on your happiness you have to allow yourself to be cared for in the specific ways he expresses his own nurturing emotions.

So how does a man show you you're the one for him? It all boils down to the three P's. Proclaim, Protect, and Provide.

First, the proclaiming part. He wants to show the world this woman is mine, because he doesn't want to lose you to someone else. It's kind of like marking his territory. He'll put his arm around you in public and will introduce you in a way that shows people you're someone special to him.

If you like him and he's proclaiming you're a special someone to anyone he introduces you to, let him do so. There's no harm in words and that weird feeling you get could be your fear more than anything else. Don't let fear override what could be a great relationship with a man, because it could push him away and you're back where you started, wondering where all the good men are at.

Second, you'll notice his protective nature. He'll show concern about your well-being, maybe offer to go car shopping with you to make sure you get the best price or want to help fix things around your house.

Keep an eye out for behaviours like that and be gracious. By rejecting them you reject a fundamental part of how he shows he cares. Tell him, "Thank you, you're such a great man," and watch his chest puff out with pride. Nothing makes him feel manlier than being able to keep the woman he cares about safe and secure.

This third point might be the one that makes you the most uncomfortable if your identity is wrapped up in being a strong independent woman - providing. Understand, we're still homo sapiens and our ancestors, early homo sapiens, survived due to a fundamental dynamic – teamwork. When our species evolved into creation 200,000 years ago we understood that unless we combined our strengths we wouldn't survive. So the men, being more powerful in physical stature than women, went out and used their brute force to kill and bring back larger animals to provide us with enough food and help sustain not only us, but the children we made.

Keep your bank account and assets, your independent hobbies and friends; nobody is saying you should surrender your life to a man. But let him support you in his own way; it's how he expresses how much he cares. We might not have as much body hair and our foreheads are much smoother now, but we're still part caveman in our innate behaviours and instincts. When we recognize that a man still needs to practice the three P's to feel bonded to us we can relax our stranglehold on independence and see that allowing him to treat us well is an act of grace, not weakness.

Your unease is your issue to deal with, not something you should use as an excuse to retrain his behaviour so you'll feel better about situations that make you feel uncomfortable. If you react to that feeling and use it to change what he wants to do for you, he'll feel less attached and look for a woman he can love in a way that feels natural to him. What you'll end up with is a guy, because guys are happy not fulfilling the role of a real man.

So what do you do with that feeling of discomfort when you're out to dinner and he reaches for the check? Change it to gratitude. If he's paid the last three dinners certainly reach for your wallet, but if he insists be gracious. Look him in the eye and say with full sincerity, "Thank you, I appreciate this." Say nothing about how you're uncomfortable, oh you wish he wouldn't, geez you're not used to being treated so much, boy does this feel awkward. Ladies, you're hurting his ears.

All he's looking for when he's doing this is simple acknowledgement. We all want to be proud of ourselves, and every action we take has a payback. He's doing this as much for his own satisfaction as he is to please you. There's no such thing as true altruism; when you do something nice you're getting an emotional reward too. So allow him his moment, his nature, his method of showing he cares about you.

Another common mistake women make with men is self-abasement. I do it just as often as you, but I never let the words pass my lips. Our words don't only effect those who hear them; they affect our minds too. The more you say something the more you believe it's true and if you love yourself, you'll stop trying to convince yourself you're not amazing. At the very least, don't deflect his compliments.

When he says, "You look nice," don't point out what you don't like about your hair, makeup, clothing, or shape of your body. Ever. There is absolutely no point to that, and in reality there's a good chance he won't notice anyway. Men aren't made to see details the way we are because the primary care of a growing human being isn't part of their make-up. They're designed to perceive when our faces are happy and be able to read a map better than we are, but noticing fine details is part of a woman's DNA. So despite that flutter in your stomach screaming at you to reject his kind words, shush and just look him in the eye, smile sweetly, and say, "What a nice thing to say, thank you!" Then take his hand and have a wonderful date.

Remember, there's nothing wrong with leaving yourself up on that pedestal. A man wants to be with a woman he's proud of, and he wants his woman to be proud of herself too.

The key here is not rejecting the positive things someone nudges your way. When someone gives you a compliment and you come back with a self-negating statement, you leave the bearer feeling a bit empty inside. When someone gives you a compliment it rewards them emotionally, knowing they said something kind that should make you feel better about yourself. The fact that you don't shouldn't be flipped back at them because it'll only smack them in the face and leave them feeling a little shell-shocked. Be gracious,   say thank you, and do something else to help deal with any nagging voices in your head saying you don't deserve this, like meditation or therapy.

Love is not always comfortable, and that's where the growth lies. Your discomfort in the face of goodness indicates where you need to rise and become a new person, one who can not only give love but accept it too. Make this part of your odyssey, and you'll find an amazing man who will share your journey with you.

STEP 6
Intimacy

When we look at intimacy as a by-product of sexuality we are missing a huge part of what true love is.

Intimacy should be what brings you to the gates of sexuality, not a side-effect.

CHAPTER 41

Making Love With Your Soul

I PUT MY HEAD ON HIS SHOULDER and tucked it into the spot that now felt as familiar as the back of my hand. He gently stroked my hair, and I listened to his breathing, relaxing into the rhythm of his body as his chest rose and fell under the arm I'd wrapped around him. I melted into the comfort we'd developed, savouring our habit of quiet snuggles followed by talking, and then more cuddles, like parentheses of tenderness around the torrent of words we exchanged.

I leaned back and looked into his face.

"I'm very fond of you, you know," I said, gazing deep into his hazel eyes.

"Me too" he replied warmly, gathering me in closer. I smiled as my heart swelled with affection and snuggled back into my favourite place, where it was warm and sweet and oh so right. It all felt like love, but surely it was too soon to tell.

After a while I leaned back, and we talked. About our day, about people we'd come across, about our lives. Every once in a while I kissed his face, my lips drawn to the tender spot on his cheekbone near the corner of his eye because it was safe there, far from the lips I wanted to seek. He closed his eyes and tilted his head slightly, a small "mmm" of appreciation escaping him every time my lips made contact. He never tried to make my kisses land on his mouth; he was waiting for permission for that.

"You have to go now," I said eventually, smiling. It was a familiar line, one communicating that as much as I enjoyed our time together we had to say goodbye to gather our wits again and avoid getting caught up in the moment lest we forget to use our brains. Besides, no kissing meant no sleepovers either, giving us time to reflect and miss each other between visits.

For the first time I felt in control of the pace, and I loved it. No more rushing into bed because I didn't know how to proceed otherwise. No more letting a guy's interests lead the way.

No more being in the passenger seat when it came to love.

I was the captain of this ship now, and it didn't just feel good; it felt amazing. I was opening up in whole new ways, my heart and soul swelling bigger than ever. I could sense myself expand and fill the space between us, and I could feel him growing into me, like two trees whose roots intertwined underground.

I walked him to the door and he turned to draw me into his arms, rocking gently as he held me close. I wrapped my arms around his neck and pressed into him, thinking if I ever found a zipper in his chest I'd probably open it and climb inside, just to get closer.

I pressed my lips onto the delicate spot on his cheek again, kissing my affection into him, then stepped back and watched him go. I had a lot to think about.

CHAPTER 42

Laying a Solid Foundation

DO YOU KNOW WHAT HAPPENS when you take kissing and sexuality out of the equation for the first three months? You both become resourceful when communicating affection and appreciation. "Necessity is the mother of invention," said a long-forgotten soul, and it's true. If you make it necessary for someone to show what you mean to them in any form other than sexuality, they seek creative ways to display just how deep their feelings run.

Tenderness, nurturing, and communication are qualities you'll both have to develop to relay what's happening in your mind and in your heart. Exploration, both inside your relationship and together in the real world, becomes how you get to know each other, instead of closing yourself off in your house for sex, followed by cuddles and sleep.

There are three factors that best predict the level of love achieved in any relationship, and these three months are the perfect time to see if you can foster them together.

1 - Responsiveness: How kindly you react to each other is the single greatest indicator of whether your love will thrive. Being conscious of how you acknowledge your partner along with how willing you are to meet even their smallest needs is the best way you can put this to practice.

When he calls your name look at him and say, "Yes?" with your full attention. If you're feeling grumpy and reply in a gruff way, take responsibility for that and let him know it has nothing to do with him. "I'm sorry, that wasn't about you. I was just thinking about how frustrated I am with my boss," followed by a touch not only erases any negative reaction he might have experienced, but the communication and affection will help develop intimacy. We are all sensitive beings, so be kind and clear at all times.

Find ways to practice kindness. Get to know him and figure out how you can bring a smile to his face. He has a sweet tooth? Keep his favourite treats on hand, but hidden away so you can have the pleasure of seeing his face light up when you bring them out. We say, "It's the little things that matter," but we don't think as much about them as we should. Those dozen little acts of kindness a day add up in someone's sense of being loved.

Should he be doing the same for you? Yes, he should respond with kind attention when you say his name, although know that if it's during a football game (or whatever he's into) it may take a moment for his brain to register you're talking to him. Keep in mind that while a woman's brain is highly capable of multitasking, men's brains tend to focus on one thing at any given time. So if you need to say something while he's distracted give him a moment to switch gears and turn his full attention to you.

As for the little things, some men prefer to do fewer, bigger gestures instead of a multitude of smaller things, so pay attention to what he's doing rather than focussing on what he isn't. Remember, perception is reality, and we're not always 100% right. Start writing down everything he does for a few weeks to see if maybe you're overlooking his efforts before you become upset.

If you practice kindness and it's not returned you can predict this same behaviour in the long run. Don't stick around and suffer in a relationship empty of even the simplest sweetnesses. (Yes, I made up a word.) There's plenty of time to find a man who will reciprocate, but life is too short to stick around for someone who can't offer you the basics in love.

2 – Understanding: We all want to be understood, but too often I hear people in relationships complain "He (she) just doesn't get me!" before figuring out their partner first. Why is it fair to seek to be understood without taking the time to get someone else? If you want a great relationship it's your responsibility to understand the human being in front of you, and you always have the power to lead by example. Once you've done your homework it's fair to fight for them to delve deeper into your brain too.

I like to say, "With understanding comes compassion," and I feel true love is borne out of compassion, so dig deep. Figure out this man's love language so you can respond in a way that'll make sense to his heart. Delve into his past so you can better understand why he is who he is today: the good, the bad, and the ugly. Remember, this is your time to really get to know him. If something scares you off, it's better to realize it sooner rather than later.

Be sure to be yourself too. This is his time as much as yours to answer an important question: Is this relationship going to be right for me? Open up about your needs and dreams, what your fears are, what makes you happy, worried, sad. When my husband and I did couples counselling before getting married we did an exercise called peeling the onion, where we talked about those things until we couldn't think of anything else to disclose. Open the door to each other's soul and peek inside. If you can both accept what's there, that's a great sign.

Don't allow yourself to fall in love with a stranger. If he's not willing to talk about who he is, that's a red flag that shouldn't be ignored. Keep looking for a man who's willing to share his heart with you.

3 - Respect: Find out what his needs are and respect them. If he works long hours it's because he needs to feel useful and proactive, so if that's a problem for you either learn to accept it or find someone whose lifestyle is more compatible to your needs. Don't stay and complain about not seeing him enough. If he rushes home because he wants to watch Monday Night Football and yell at the TV to blow off some steam, respect that and yell with him or find something to keep you occupied in the meantime. I'll sit beside my husband and work on my laptop as a compromise between his wish to have me close by and my desire to get some work done.

And of course he should give your needs the same level of respect. If you need at least three hours a week of girl time he should be gracious and not make you feel guilty about not being with him. If you want pretty nails because they make you happy he shouldn't be snippy about the money you spend at the salon.

Learn his boundaries and hold them as dear to you as your own. He likes having quiet TV time when it's playoff season? Find something to do when the game is on. He's not a social butterfly like you? Only ask him to accompany you to events you classify as important.

He should respect your boundaries too. Maya Angelou once said to Oprah, "Anyone who doesn't accept no for an answer is trying to control you." Remember this and pay attention to whether he's respecting the limits you lay out before him. It's up to you to remove them when you're ready, and if he tries to convince you you're wrong to have them he's not honoring your feelings. Don't let this man be the love of your life.

Be fine-tuned to what he's saying, and equally important, what he's not saying. If you're spilling your guts and he doesn't share anything about himself, maybe it's best to move on and find someone more willing to communicate. Love is about more than just the feelings between you; it's the ability to give each other a safe place to be yourself, warts and all, and to be accepted.

CHAPTER 43

Water His Garden and Watch Him Grow

MEN ARE SUCH SENSITIVE BEINGS, but we've been fooled by society into believing otherwise. When I give classes on how to understand men I ask, "What do you want from a man? Reassurance, support, kindness, displays of devotion, grand gestures? And what do you think men want?" Without fail women reply men want two things: sex and food. That's it.

But guess what? Men want the same things we do. They too need reassurance, support, kindness, displays of devotion, and grand gestures, but because the cultural message has been that boys are tough and don't cry, we forget they have feelings too.

How do we know men feel just as deeply as we do? Researchers at MindLab examined the physiological response from both men and women while viewing images they rated either funny, exciting, blissful, or heartwarming. While the study found men had slightly stronger emotional reactions to funny, exciting, and blissful, their emotional response doubled women's when it came to heartwarming.

And yet when asked afterward to rate their feelings in a survey and were subsequently asked about their answers, 67% of men later confessed they underrated their emotions. Men's feelings have been undervalued and pushed aside for so long, they themselves are unsure of how freely they can communicate them.

Since research has proven men's feelings run just as deep as ours, we can use that knowledge to make significant deposits in their emotional bank accounts. It's not hard to make a deposit either. Look for the little or big things he does for you, and let him know you noticed. Did he fix your leaky faucet? "I love that you're such a great handyman," will have him reaching for his toolbox as soon as the washing machine breaks down. If he brings you a trinket because he thought you'd appreciate it, "You're so attentive, I love how thoughtful you are!" will have you on his mind all day long, wondering what else he can do to show how important you are to him.

Compliment the qualities he shows through his words and actions, and you'll see him stepping forward to reinforce your positive impression of him. Men thrive and flourish under our affirmative words, so don't be cheap with them. If you want love to flow freely in your relationship lead by example, giving praise when something good happens. Wouldn't you want to live up to someone's favourable impression of you?

And for goodness' sakes, ladies, let a man be a man! If he wants to open doors for you he's responding to something inside that says chivalry isn't dead. Don't kill it for him by refusing to let him treat you like a lady, because those little things count in his mind. Give him the precious smile he's looking for, and say, "Thank you, you're so sweet!" We seek little moments and ways to boost our self-esteem through our good deeds, and if you take these away from him he'll look for a woman who'll give him those opportunities to feel good about himself.

CHAPTER 44

7 Qualities a Real Man is Looking for in a Woman

I'M NOT GOING TO LIE TO YOU... I sometimes feel I channel this stuff, like I'm tapped into a source pouring ideas in my brain. This is one of them, and every time I talk to men about these seven qualities the feedback is the same: "I hadn't thought about it so thoroughly, but all those points are valid and I can't think of anything to add to this list." So ladies, pay attention because when all is said and done a woman embodying these seven qualities will be the one who'll warm the heart of a real man.

1 – A Woman Who Is Emotionally Strong: Did you know little boys cry more than girls? Males are sensitive their entire lives, but we squash their emotions with societal expectations. Again, big boys don't cry, right? Whereas girls have always been encouraged and even expected to cry. It's not fair, and it's no wonder males have higher rates addiction; they haven't been allowed the opportunity to let their feelings run their course like we have.

Men appreciate a woman who is strong enough to have the patience, nurturing, and love to see them through their own emotional tough times and allow them to grow through them.

They appreciate the safe place you provide to become a better man. Love is about giving space without judgement and offering forgiveness when the journey takes us down rough roads, and being able to evolve together is what truly bonds two people in love.

Not that you won't have your own moments where you need his emotional support. It just means you have the ability to be ready, willing, and able to support him when he needs it too. We have to be able to take turns being the pillar of strength in the relationship.

2 – A Woman Who Has Weaknesses: I know it sounds counterintuitive to the first point, but I like a little shock value now and then. Here's what I mean by this: A man is protective by nature and still has an instinct to defend his mate. He wants to be with a woman who has vulnerabilities he can protect and nurture, because they help him feel needed in the relationship. A woman who doesn't allow a man to take care of her in any way gives the impression there's no role for him in her life.

I'm not saying you should quit your job and become dependent on him. I'm saying let him kill those spiders, even if you could kill them yourself. Find something he, and only he, can tend to for you. Big or small, there has to be something he's the man for the job in your life. At the very least, allow him to be the one who can hold you and say everything will be all right when you're upset.

Being able to lean on each other exclusively in some areas, no matter how minor, cements his sense of companionship.

This gives him the impression he has a special place with you, growing his love and commitment.

3 – A Woman Who Is Feminine: Let's face it, a man just wants to feel like a man, and having a woman by his side who can play up her femininity helps him achieve just that. He'll still love to see you slap on rubber boots and muck through the trenches with him, but when you come out of the bathroom all dolled up for a night on the town he's going to say to himself, "That's right, that's a woman who shows the world I'm her man!"

Watch his chest puff out, his eyes light up with appreciation, and how he smiles when he sees you because you've made him feel like a million and one dollars just by looking like a million yourself.

4 – A Woman Who Doesn't Need Him: And by need I mean clingy. Repeat after me, a man is a prettier version of a caveman. His instinct to hunt and chase is still there. It's just being exercised in ways like finding the perfect deal on a car. But that's not all he wants to chase, and a woman who keeps the hunt going excites his brain.

Part of his thrill happens in the effort it takes to convince a woman she needs him around. Men love women they can occasionally pursue, and giving him the moon one day and taking a personal day the next keeps him guessing and thinking.

If you had your favourite treat every single hour of every single day, would you tire of it? It's the same for men. When your need for him isn't constant it remains something of a novelty, and he appreciates it all the more when you turn to him and say, "I need you right now."

Love is a verb, and it's found in the things you do for one another. Give him breaks in terms of loving you, and he'll dish it out that much stronger when you need it from him.

5 – A Woman Who Will Challenge Him: Men are curious by nature and love being with women who regularly expand who they are. This keeps them from feeling the relationship is mundane, and they love the added spice every time you introduce something new.

It doesn't matter what you pursue and educate yourself on, what matters is how much it fires you up talking about it. Bringing home the new and exciting things you're filling your mind and soul with gives him an added opportunity to expand his own mind.

Having opinions on what you learn and what he shares with you will keep him on his toes. Plus, the thrill of watching you evolve will inspire deeper feelings and give him the sense he too can change, and that change is okay and nurtured in your relationship.

6 – A Woman Who Is Confident: This is numero uno when it comes to attracting and keeping a good man. Men don't want to spend every minute with a woman trying to convince her she's as great as they already believe. They appreciate a woman who knows her own value and qualities and allows a man to be the icing on her cake, instead of forcing him to be a constant cheerleader.

Men want to find out what makes you amazing and love you for it, so be confident in your worth, and allow a man to love you the way you are. If you're lacking this, nothing else will matter because you don't love yourself enough to be loved. If you need to, practice the fake it 'til you make it method by not verbalizing any insecurities. You'll find they'll fade into the background while you let him love you.

And I don't mean shed all of your insecurities, although wouldn't that be great? I have insecurities too, but I'll show 1/1,000 of them to my husband because I don't want to discolour his view of me with my own skewed vision. We are our own worst enemies, I'm well aware of that, but you don't have to push someone else's impression of you in the gutter just because of your own beliefs that your hair is too frizzy or your tummy doesn't tuck enough.

Confidence is the ability to shoulder your own self- image and move forward despite anything you think holds you back. It's the ability to let your goals override your uncertainty, to charge forward with power instead of reacting to doubt. Behave confidently despite any nagging voices in your head.

Step into the exquisiteness he sees: Rise up and be loved. Let go of your fears, and advance into a space where you are cherished and appreciated. I know you want to.

7 – A Woman Who Is Independent: A real man is out there in the world, conquering. He wants to be with a woman who is doing her own conquering, whether it's in business or pleasure. Being with a woman who has ambition to succeed and independent passions gives him peace of mind, knowing she's not hinging her whole world on him, and the knowledge she's keeping herself fulfilled while he's taking care of his own fulfillment gives him comfort.

I'm not saying don't plan to be home when he is if that's what you both like. But maintain your own interests aside from your relationship with him, and have something that rounds you out so all your financial, mental, and emotional eggs aren't in one basket. A man who loves you will want you to feel like a whole person.

Emotionally strong, yet vulnerable. Feminine yet powerful. Intelligent and confident. Embody these qualities, and you will become a woman who can not only win over any amazing man, but be able to achieve and adapt to anything you want from life. You'll love yourself so much that love will not just flow, but gush towards you, as per the laws of attraction. Intimacy is love in its purest form, and it can only be shared when your doors are wide open to everything life has to offer.

STEP 7

Love

If love was a bicycle, faith would be one of the wheels Committing to anyone takes a leap of faith. Choose the right man to grow with, and your courage will be rewarded with the most amazing love you could imagine.

CHAPTER 45

Here is Where I Rest My Soul

THIS IS IT, I THOUGHT. *Tonight's the night!* I browsed the card selection at Hallmark until I found what I was looking for. "The best gift of all!" it said on the outside, the black background punctuated by shiny balloons and streamers. Inside it was blank; I'd be inserting my own special message later.

I brought my card to the counter and paid, smiling to myself as I considered what this small piece of paper would unlock. Tonight wasn't only going to be our first kiss; it would be the first step through a door of infinite possibilities.

I went home and prepared for our date. He had no idea what I was planning, no clue that tonight we were going to kiss for the first time. For all he knew I was coming over to cuddle and hang out, something we'd done a million times before. I pulled the card from my purse and opened it. Inside I wrote four words: Me. All of me.

When I arrived at his house he met me at the door, gathering me in his arms to hold me close. Nobody had ever hugged me as long or as intimately as he did, and I knew I wanted this for as long as I could have it. I laid my head on his shoulder while he rocked gently, resting my soul as time stood still. I couldn't wait to give him my card.

We sat on the couch and I pulled it out of my purse, putting it in his hands. He looked at me.

"For me?"

"Happy birthday," I said, hiding my nervousness behind a playful smile. He opened it, and a small huff escaped his lips as his breath left his body. He looked at me intensely, his eyes suddenly ablaze.

"Can I kiss you?"

I had imagined his first kiss already: tentative, slow, maybe even hesitant.

"Yes" I replied, and the moment the word left my lips he closed the distance between us, cupping his hand on the side of my face and finding my lips with his before my brain could fully register what was happening. I found the surprise thrilling, his lack of hesitation forever sealing my opinion of him as a real man, one who was ever respectful yet able to dive in and claim what was his.

His lips were perfect: soft, seeking, passionate, making this kiss the most sublime kiss I'd ever experienced.

His kisses still are, and every morning and every night, (and sometimes in between), I tenderly and lovingly kiss this man, now my husband. He's taught me what it means to love and grow as a human, what it means to feel someone's soul when they hold you tight. He is my muse, my partner, my playmate, my friend, my fart buddy. My everything.

CHAPTER 46
Now the Real Work

YOU'VE BEEN MEDITATING, you clarified what you wanted, and you went out there and found him by weeding through the muck and finding the diamond in the rough. By resisting your animal impulses you found yourself in a relationship with a real man, letting him get to know you before allowing the true intimacy you developed to happen. It's been an incredible journey.

But guess what? Now the actual work is just beginning.

Sure, it's a lot of work to find the perfect man, but now you want to keep him. Now the hard part starts because you're both bringing forth baggage, seeking to unpack and create a relationship that's different from the ones you've left behind. Now is when you have to understand that love is a verb, found not just in what you feel but what you say and do.

Love is overcoming anger and misunderstanding, it's your patience and forgiveness and those little things you do just for him. It's in "I'm sorry" and the minutes you spend meditating to bring a greater measure of peace and contentment to the relationship. Love is biting your tongue or giving praise, it's driving out of your way or staying a bit longer, speaking a foreign Love Language or developing more maturity. It's in taking turns being the one to hold it all together.

Love is a feeling, yes, but more than anything love is a behaviour.

CHAPTER 47
Love is…Communication

MY EX-HUSBAND AND I would have moments where we'd realize this last fight was the result of a lack of communication. "Read my mind!" he'd complain in a cutely exasperated way, and we'd laugh.

We can't read each other's minds, but we can be clear when communicating our needs, and men certainly appreciate the guidance. In my opinion, the best way to resolve a fight is to not have it in the first place, and this technique helps you both feel like you're getting what you want from each other.

One of the biggest fights couples have happens when she's upset about something and he's offering advice instead of comfort. You know the scenario. You're complaining about traffic on the way home from work and it was the shit cherry on your shit day, and he's pointing out you could have taken a different route or left at a different time, and you yell:

"OH MY GOD YOU'RE NOT LISTENING TO ME!!"

Then he yells something back and you find yourself hollering that maybe if he'd (fill in the blank) things wouldn't be so crappy, and now you're in a huge fight.

Which didn't need to happen.

What did you actually want? You wanted him to listen to you vent, then put his arms around you and say, "Everything is going to be okay," didn't you? But he didn't know that. You have to teach him what you need until his ability to predict the future based on experience takes over and he understands you automatically.

The comforting hug technique was foreign to me until I learned about it in couples therapy, but a huge light went off in my brain. It made sense that a good dose of oxytocin would be the perfect remedy to a stressful event, but the obstacle lies in whether your partner knows how important this is to you. It confounded me for the longest time that my hubby didn't automatically do this, especially once we'd heard about it, but I became creative in my problem solving and learned how to teach him.

Me: Upset about something.

Him: Clueless about what to do, therefore reverting to throwing out solutions.

Me: Turn to him and simply say, "I need you to put your arms around me and tell me everything is going to be okay." (The key here is to not turn my anger and frustration on him.)

Him: Puts his arms around me and says, "Everything is going to be okay, baby," and feels relieved he's doing something that actually helps.

Me: Feeling comforted and happy.

See? It really can be that simple, and men love it when we simplify things rather than hope they'll read our minds. Some women say, "He should just know," when I talk about being ultra-clear about our needs, but that's not fair. Teach him, and do so patiently. I've been with my man for over 12 years and I'll still say to him, "I'm having a bad day, I need you to put your arms around me and tell me everything is going to be okay." Regardless of how crazy his day is, he'll mentally drop everything to give me the moment I need because I made it easy for him to help me feel better. I feel comforted and he feels like a great husband (aka hero) and everybody's winning.

I read a great quote on Twitter that summed it up perfectly: "Love is a very simple thing. Let's complicate it with expectations." Trust me, when you boil it down the vast majority of fights revolve around unmet expectations. Simplify your needs by communicating, and you'll cut your fights in half. Don't expect him to just know how to help you. Be a gentle guide and help him learn how to deal with your emotional tides.

CHAPTER 48

The Art of Sorry

THERE'S AN ART FORM TO APOLOGIES, and learning it completely changed my relationship. Fights were resolved faster and happened less often because I became proactive in fixing them, sometimes even before any words left my mouth.

Too often we let our egos do the talking, but your ego isn't interested in having a functional relationship; it's only interested in being right. Take a step back and ask yourself what's important: a peaceful relationship or never being wrong. You can't have both.

So if you're willing to learn the art of peace, continue reading. This chapter is for you.

Below are the 5 steps I learned which helped me stop having fights with my man. Sometimes I used all 5 at once, sometimes just one, but they're all invaluable for a harmonious relationship.

1 – Stop: The moment your disagreement escalates to raised voices, stop and leave. Go to another room, get off the phone as nicely as you can, do whatever you can to halt the progression. Anger and ego are taking over, and nothing productive will happen from this point. Two cool heads are needed to fix a problem, and one or both of you are losing yours.

So take a time out and cool down; you'll be much more productive once rational thought is injected into the situation.

2 – Balance: This is the last technique I learned but the best one for nixing fights before they start. Every time I had something to complain about I took a moment and asked myself, "Before I get into this, is there anything I should apologize for first? Have I covered all my responsibilities? Have I avoided being bitchy for no reason? (Damn you, hormones!) Have I been perfect in my responses to his Love Language? Have I been completely honest about everything?"

If I came up with one thing, like leaving a messy kitchen, letting the lawn get wild, or not picking up dog poop (all things that are on my chore list around the house) I used it to balance what was on my mind. I forgave him because I wasn't asking forgiveness for my own transgressions. I balanced his imperfections with my own, and it emotionally fixed the problem for me.

We spend so much time focusing on what our partner is doing without taking a moment to ask ourselves, *What can I do better?* Be fair in your relationship, and understand that his imperfections are likely matched by yours. Focus on what you could change before trying to fix him. You'll reduce the number of fights you have and benefit from his desire to keep up with how awesome you are.   Remember, the only person you can change is you, and when you lead by example people tend to follow.

3 – Apologize: It's so much easier than people think, because saying "I'm sorry" is simply acknowledging what I could've done differently, nothing more. We had a fight, and I lost my cool? I'm sorry I lost my cool, I should've handled that better. I'm sorry for acting jealous or bitchy. I'm sorry for not cleaning the kitchen before you got home and leaving a mess. I got so good at saying I'm sorry, my husband had nothing to complain about because I was quick to call out my own brain farts first.

After a blowout search your brain for what you could've done better, and lay them out on the table. After that you're clear to walk away, knowing you've recognized and acknowledged your part.

One eye opening thing my husband has taught me is that the truth hurts. I hated when he said that but it resonated in my mind, and I began to analyze the things he said. And you know what? The truth does hurt. When he said something that rubbed my ego wrong I stopped rejecting his words and mulled them over instead, and more often than not what he was saying had some truth to it. I had flaws.

There's absolutely nothing wrong with admitting where you went wrong. In fact it's so freaking noble it takes a huge amount of oomph out of any fight. Now that the fight can't be about him getting you to see where you're wrong, all that's left is for him to acknowledge where he went wrong.

And there's something deflating to a fight when you're willing to come forth, own, and apologize for your behaviours. Fights contain a lot of defensive emotions, filled with good old, "don't be willing to point the finger at me without looking at your own BS first," attitudes. So the moment you admit where you messed up, what's left? In my experience once I took care of my half of the equation I didn't care as much anymore. There was nothing for him to say about me, and if he didn't want to take responsibility for his own actions there was nothing I could do about that.

But I found that by putting my weaknesses on the table my man apologized for his own transgressions, and peace was restored. It's hard for someone to be angry when the person they love is asking for forgiveness and showing grace.

What if he never takes responsibilities for his own wrongdoings? Then you've got a guy on your hands, and you know what to do about that: Say goodbye and find a man who's grown up enough to admit when he's wrong.

Now here's the secret to crafting an apology that will come across as so sincere not an ounce of defensiveness will be tossed back at you: Completely cut out the word "but". If you use that word consider everything you said before it to be negated in your partner's mind, and all they'll want to do is prove why your but is wrong. There's no point saying you're sorry if you're adding the word but in there. The fight will just continue because what follows but is usually you. Now you've put him back on the defensive, and the response is "Yeah, but you…" and you're still fighting instead of resolving.

Take the time to really think about what you'll say when you apologize, and don't start talking until the word "but" has been eliminated in your mind.

And when all is said and done, be sure to give each other a loooooong hug. Remember, oxytocin is released during physical touch, and now is the time to use your body's tools to help heal your emotions. Because of oxytocin's effects you'll regain a sense of the warm fuzzies for each other and forget some of the negativity that was exchanged before you made up. It's the hug that seals the deal and brings you closer again, deepening your intimacy once more. Make sure it lasts at least 20 seconds to get the full effects.

4 – Change: You can't control anybody but yourself (I've tried, doesn't work), and by acknowledging your own faults today you empower yourself to be a better person tomorrow. Think about what you're apologizing for, and try to do better going forward. While nobody expects you to change overnight baby steps are always better than none. If your partner stays in the dark ages despite your growth you may outgrow him, but the benefit will be attracting a better quality man next time, one who's equally willing to evolve.

As Oprah says, "When you know better, you do better."

5 – Lead: This is the most important step of them all: Lead by example. Hubby and I used to fight a lot, but that subsided when I stopped trying to change him and focused on myself instead. By becoming more humble about my faults we both felt like we stopped hitting brick walls, and he was so happy he followed suit.

The most effective way to change how people behave around you is to change your own behaviour first, then sit back and enjoy the ripple effects. Meditation plays a huge role in how you feel about conflict too; for me it took the desire to fight right out of my system. I started meditating just about daily, and as I reflect back I realize we haven't had a single fight since. Amazing. Kindness, consideration, and a ridiculous amount of happiness and harmony has replaced the angst we used to experience. We have a great relationship today because I put all my energy into becoming a better person and appreciating the things he did for me. When people feel they can step forward and become better on their own accord they'll usually do so, especially when they see how happy you become when you do it first.

CHAPTER 49

Be an Agent of Peace

TAKE CARE OF YOURSELF, your inner sense of peace, and grow the love you have for your own heart and humanity. Meditate every day and ooze so much contentment the people around you can't help picking up what you're putting down.

You can only dish out what's inside you, remember that. If you're picking up stressors all day long without easing them with an amygdala shrinking exercise like meditation, all you'll be dishing out is stress, anger, and frustration.

If you balance life with a minimum of ten minutes of meditation a day not only will you find inner peace, but the people in your life will experience peace just by being around you. They'll love and appreciate your calm, loving presence, and you'll rack up the reasons to feel grateful, further perpetuating all those wondrous feelings you're developing.

Relationships rarely go sideways; they either get better or worse with time because as human beings we're too dynamic to stay exactly the same year after year. It's up to you to guide your current or next love relationship, but one thing I know for certain: Every day we get to choose which way we want to go in life, and today is always the perfect day to choose something better for yourself.

I'm happy today because of the steps I took in this book. I wish the same for every woman on this planet, and I thank the Universe for any positive change I may have helped you create in your own life.

Namaste, my sister! Go forth and create a ton of love.

CHAPTER 50
What About Online Dating?

YOU PROBABLY NOTICED BY NOW I haven't touched on the subject of online dating yet. I mean, in today's world shouldn't a section about dating websites be the first chapter, not the last? But here's the thing… if you're reading this book because you can't figure out how to find a man who'll stay and play instead of play and go, maybe starting from scratch is the way to go at this point.

We've been lulled by our culture to believe satisfaction is something we find out there instead of something we cultivate for ourselves. Every form of media we see guides us to look outside ourselves for what we need. If you're lonely, connect with people on Facebook or have a chat with someone of a dating site. A nicer car will surely make you happier. Buying that whitening toothpaste will increase your attractiveness.

We spend so much time immersed in computer screens, and it becomes easy to dismiss a potential partner because there are hundreds more once we log onto a dating site. There's a ton of men looking for a woman to give them a chance, but we're training them to have shorter and shorter attention spans because our own is so fleeting and our requirements so low. Women succumb to the cultural pressure to give it all before they know who a guy is and move on and start over again when they feel he's not living up to their expectations.

If this is you, it's time to bring it back to the basics. Get off the dating sites, put on headphones and some meditative music, and bring your focus back to yourself. Build what you're looking for from the inside out, because trying to fill the void from the outside in isn't working. Fill yourself up with love, bring your intuition to life, and find what makes you happy and fulfilled.

See, here's the thing: If you're feeling lonely and don't have enough love in your life, if you have unresolved pain from your upbringing that's created a dialogue in your head saying, "I'm not good enough," getting into a relationship is like taking morphine to treat a gunshot wound. Sure, the pain is dulled and you feel good for a moment, but the gunshot wound is still there, and once the morphine wears off that pain comes back.

Remember how I talked about oxytocin and dopamine flushing your body in the initial stages of a relationship? That's your morphine. But finding someone to love you is only half the equation. You need to love yourself just as much as you'd want a partner to love you or at least bring yourself close to that level first. By operating on yourself before going out there and looking for someone to spend your life with you bring yourself closer to being with the right man.

Once you start the healing process you'll find the man who'll help you the rest of the way by creating a space of greater love for you to grow into. But you need to begin in earnest before your frequency can attract the right person to take this journey with you. Because like attracts like, the more pain you're in when looking for a relationship the more likely you are to attract someone suffering from the same deep wounds. But if you're on a healing path, a path of self- love and care and focus on functional happiness and satisfaction, you're likely to attract a man who can travel a wondrous journey with you.

Now, let's look at how to tackle online dating in a way that'll attract the right kind of man! Here are 4 things to remember when creating your online profile.

1. **Make your photo and description representative.** If you have a favourite sports team, have a profile picture that shows you at a game. If you're an outdoorsy sort of woman, use a photo of you on your favourite hiking trail. Don't use sexy photos, because what you'll attract are guys flipping through pictures looking to answer the question, *Would I tap that?* Instead, attract a man who's looking to answer the question *Can I live with her?* by showing you doing your favourite activity. A man will be drawn to a woman he can connect with, and since like attracts like he's looking for someone who loves what he does. Be descriptive about who you are, but stay away from words that leave the impression you're just there

for a good time. Talk about your qualities, personality, and likes, and leave it at that. The goal is to attract a man who's looking for a woman, not a guy looking for a girl.

2. **Be honest about your intentions.** Don't be shy about stating what sort of relationship you're looking

3. for. If you want a long term committed relationship saying so from the get-go will eliminate guys who are just looking for something fun and easy. Don't waste your time or theirs by being vague about your reasons for being online.

4. **Say a little something vulnerable.** I recently helped a client create her Match profile, and I had her include the line "I love to cook and bake, even if I do burn things from time to time." Having an element of humanity makes you more real and touches a special part of a man's heart.

5. **Don't stick to just one site.** Men are everywhere, wondering where all the good women are. Don't be afraid to create profiles on multiple sites, because you never know where the man you're looking for will be next.

6. **Don't reply to someone unless it's obvious he's read your profile.** There are a lot of guys out there looking for the woman who'll settle for a minimal amount of effort. Don't fall for good looking or good

on paper. Stay available for the man who'll put in the effort to get to know you from the very beginning.

A word about online dating - There are a lot of guys trolling dating sites looking for women who lack self-esteem and assertive qualities. They are the ones sending pics of them in their underwear (or dick pics) soon after communicating with you. They're also the ones who get pushy and irritated when you don't respond to them quickly and give what they demand. As soon as this happens block them from communicating with you. That's it. You don't need to explain anything because you were clear   on your profile you're looking for a long term partner. And while I can understand sometimes this is a fun ego boost and tempting to follow through on, if what you're looking for is a long term, loving relationship realize this is a distraction that'll keep you from achieving your goal.

These guys are showing you from the get go what kind of people they are: someone willing to show a near stranger their schlong because for them intimacy is only a blending of bodies and not a union of hearts, minds, and long term goals.

Block them at once because you want to send a clear signal to them and the Universe you're done with guys and are only interested in a man. Then, take a deep breath, be glad you averted a train wreck, and move on.

CHAPTER 51

For the Single Mamas

FIRST OF ALL, KUDOS for even devoting time to read this, I spend two hours with my single mom friends and I'm exhausted. You're working hard to be providers, then coming home to kids with hungry tummies and even hungrier arms; it's a wonder you have any time at all. But here's one thing I know from working with single moms – if you follow the advice in this book, life gets easier.

Using these communication methods on your baby- daddy can make him easier to deal with and encourage him to be a more plugged in man for his child. Implementing the grounding technique will help you sleep better at night and feel calmer in the face of everything you have to deal with day in and day out. Taking your time with getting to know the men you meet means you'll spend less time swinging in the wind trying to decide if this particular one is right for you. My goal is for you to feel like life is easier, and I'm hoping you'll use the tools in this book to accomplish that.

Should you meet a man that you think has great potential don't hesitate to ask for a background check. Someone with something to hide will balk at the notion, want to debate you on your request, and stall forever hoping he'll win you over and get you to change your mind. A man with nothing to hide, who's intent is to win the heart of a woman he feels is amazing and wants to be nothing but a supportive source for you and your kids will understand that a caring mom is a careful mom, and get it done without causing a hassle. View this as a litmus test.

If you're afraid of losing a man who's insulted that you asked for proof that he's who he says he is, rethink that notion. Fear can cost you the safety and security of your children. Is your fear getting in the way of their well-being?

Reputable daycare centers will get a background check before hiring someone. It's not a guarantee that the person they hire won't cause harm, but it's certainly a filter. Shouldn't you have just as high a standard?

Don't leave your little ones alone in the care of someone you're dating until they're old enough to understand how predators function and what constitutes bad touching, and are able to communicate with you immediately if something happens. You might think he's the best thing to ever happen to you, but trusting him with your children should take much longer to accomplish.

Dating is a tough world to navigate, and doing it while working to support and raise kids without significant help from their daddy can be hard. Go slowly, tread carefully, and stay strong. You can do this and have something amazing at the end of the day when you're smart and savvy.

Afterword

I WANT YOU TO KNOW, there's more work ahead. In a life where love and intuition are your guiding forces the man you choose will help you explore intimate love, and be your greatest teacher. So be prepared, because now the cycle of work and achievement begins again, and there's a chance it'll be hard when you begin your relationship together. But as you grow into what a great relationship requires it's going to get really interesting because you'll hit heights you never even dreamed of.

From my personal experience and coaching practice I've witnessed this cycle of difficulty and growth over and over, but it's a succession of upswings when you approach it with an open mind and heart. Calming and expanding your mind is a lifelong quest, and when you surround yourself with the right people they create challenges which help grow your intellect and spirit. The Universe gives you what you need when you need it, and you rise to the challenge and learn or you're left in the same mindset that made you unhappy in the first place. Nothing great ever came easy, ask any millionaire entrepreneur. They'll be the first to tell you that adversity was the path to their success, with each difficult turn becoming a learning experience.

Be prepared to turn hurt into cause for reflection, and open your mind to seeking the truth behind every painful experience. Don't let ego rule your thoughts and actions, but instead find opportunities to admit where you can rise and grow. If you grow so much you leave the first great man behind that's okay, it means you're growing into something better still. Life and love is about evolution, embrace it and the difficult times that lay in your path. Keep meditating and creating balance, keep growing and learning from every emotion you have, and keep encouraging growth from those who come into your life. Build every new experience on top of the last and become a leader when it comes to love and relationships.

If you need help navigating the first year together be sure to pick up my book *After the First Kiss*. Then grab a copy of *Fix That Shit*, where I help you through the sticky spots like unpacking emotional baggage, and learning how to compromise and negotiate so you both feel like you're winning.

Remember, first it gets hard, then it gets interesting. But when you choose the right man, it's always worth the effort.

About The Author

CHANTAL LIVES IN ONTARIO with her husband Dennis and two dogs, Maggie and Lulu. She is a Human Relations expert with a successful practice, helping clients learn how to find and keep a "magical" loving relationship. As a public speaker, workshop leader, private coach, writer, and frequent media contributor, Chantal is busy distributing advice far and wide in the hopes of creating loving unions that will resonate for generations. Chantal is also a member of Zonta, a UN recognized international organization of professional women working together to advance the status of women worldwide through service and advocacy.

Visit Chantal Heide at
www.canadasdatingcoach.com
You Tube – Chantal Heide
Instagram - @canadasdatingcoach
Twitter - @CanDatingCoach
Facebook – Chantal Heide, Canada's Dating Coach

References

First Things First

1. **E.** Monita. 2007. "Psychological Effects Of Forest Environments On Healthy Adults: Shinrin-yoku (forest- air bathing, walking) As a Possible Method Of Stress Reduction" http://www.ncbi.nlm.nih.gov/pubmed/17055544
2. **Roger** S. Ulrich. April27, 1984. "View Through Window May Influence Recovery From Surgery" https://mdc.mo.gov/sites/default/files/resources/2012/10/ ulrich.pdf

Step 1: Grounding

1. Sue McGreevey. January 11, 2011. "Eight Weeks to a Better Brain" http://news.harvard.edu/gazette/story/2011/01/eight- weeks-to-a-better-brain/
2. Dorothy L. Retallack. June 1973. "The Sound of Music and Plants"
3. Thian Carman. 2014. "Chickens Mad For Mozart Produce Bigger, Heavier Eggs" http://www.cbc.ca/

news/canada/nova-scotia/chickens- mad-for-mozart-produce-bigger-heavier-eggs-1.2630194
4. Masaru Emoto. 2001. "The Hidden Messages in Water"
5. David Aldridge, January 1, 2004. Case Study Designs in Music Therapy
6. Arjun Walia. November 24, 2014. "Precognition: Science Shows How or Body Reacts to Events Up to 10 Seconds Before They Happen" http:// journal.frontiersin.org/article/10.3389/ fnhum.2014.00146/abstract
7. Norman Dodge. December 18, 2007. "The Brain That Changes Itself: Stories of Personal Triumph From The Frontiers of Brain Science"

Step 3: Overcoming Fear

1. Albert Mehrabian. July 1972. "Silent Messages: Implicit Communication of Emotions and Attitudes"

(page 83) Saul McLeod. 2014 "Cognitive Dissonance" http://www.simplypsychology.org/cognitive- dissonance.html

Notes